E Spencer

The Modern Cook

And frugal housewife's compleat guide to every branch in displaying her table to

the greatest advantage

E Spencer

The Modern Cook
And frugal housewife's compleat guide to every branch in displaying her table to the greatest advantage

ISBN/EAN: 9783744796149

Printed in Europe, USA, Canada, Australia, Japan

Cover: Foto ©Lupo / pixelio.de

More available books at **www.hansebooks.com**

THE
MODERN COOK;
AND
FRUGAL HOUSEWIFE's
COMPLEAT GUIDE

To every Branch in difplaying her Table to the greateft Advantage, viz.

The Judgment of Meat at Market;

With DIRECTIONS for

Roasting,	Stewing,	Fricasseying,
Boiling,	Broiling,	and
Hashing,	Frying,	Baking:

Also for MAKING

Puddings,	Pies,	Creams,
Custards,	Tarts,	Jellies,
Cakes,	Ragouts,	Syllabubs,
Cheese Cakes,	Soups,	Wines, &c.

And several felect Papers by a Lady of Diftinction, lately deceafed, of New and in Infallible Rules to be obferved in

Pickling, | Preserving, | Brewing, &c.

BY
E. SPENCER,
Late Principal COOK to a Capital Tavern in London.

NEWCASTLE UPON TYNE:
PRINTED for the Author, 1782.

INDEX.

	Page.
DIRECTIONS for Marketing	1 to 7
—— for Roasting	7 to 20
—— for Boiling Meat	20 to 25
—— for boiling Greens, &c.	25 to 29
—— for Hashing, Stewing, &c.	29 to 58
—— for making Pyes	58 to 78
—— for making Tarts	78 to 80
—— for making Puddings	80 to 90
—— for making Dumplings	90 to 92
—— for making Broths, Soops, &c.	92 to 111
—— for Pickling	111 to 119
—— for Preserving	119 to 124
—— for Candying	124 to 126
—— for making Cakes, &c.	126 to 133
—— for making Syllabubs, &c.	133 to 135
—— for making Jellies and Jams	135 to 136
—— for made Wines, &c.	136 to 139
—— for Brewing	139 to 141
Bill of Fare for every Month	141 to 147
Gravies and Sauces	147 to 152

ERRATUM.

Page 24, 2*d line from the bottom,* *instead of* with pepper, salt, &c. *read* mace, salt, &c.

INTRODUCTION.

Directions for MARKETING, *&c.*

Shewing the Seasons of the Year for Butcher's Meat, Poultry, Fish, &c.

To chuse Venison.

THE season for Buck Venison begins in May, and is in season till All-hallows day; the Doe is in season from Michaelmas to the end of December, and sometimes to the end of January. You must wipe it quite dry with a cloth, rub it with vinegar to prevent the flies getting to it, or it will soon spoil: it is generally kept eight days before used, to make it tender and give it a fine flavour. Try the haunches or shoulders under the bones that come out, with your finger or knife, and as the scent is sweet or rank, it is new or stale; and the like of the sides in the most fleshy parts: if tainted they will look greenish in some places, or very black. Look on the hoofs, and if the clefts are very wide and rough it is old, if close and smooth it is young.

To chuse Lamb.

In chusing a Lamb's-head observe the eyes; if they are wrinkled or sunk in, it is stale; if lively and plump it is new and sweet. In a fore-quarter mind the neck-vein be of a sky-blue, then it is sweet and good; but if inclining to green or yellow, it is almost if not tainted: in a hind-quarter, if it has a faintish smell under the kidney, and the knuckle be limber, it is stale.

To chuse Mutton.

To judge of Mutton, you must look at the lean part, where the fore quarter is cut off from the hind, and it will be marbled with fat, and the lean of a dark red; consequently in perfection as it will be about five years old: but if young, it will not be so mixed in the grain; and the lean of a pale red. If the fat be inclinable to yellow, it is tainted in the feeding.

To chuse Veal.

If the bloody vein in the shoulder looks a bright red it is new killed; but if blackish, or greenish, it is stale. The loin first taints under the kidney, and the flesh if stale, will be soft and slimy.

The neck and breast taint first at the upper end, and you will perceive some dusky, yellowish, or greenish appearance, the sweetbread on the breast will be clammy, otherwise it is fresh and good.

The flesh of a bull calf is redder and firmer than that of a cow calf, and the fat harder; but always chuse quey veal.

To chuse Beef.

If Ox, and proper age, the lean will be of a darkish red, and marbled in the grain, which may be seen at the lean part of the thin end of the surloin, or at the cutting of the fore-chain. The fat of Cow Beef is whiter, and the lean a pale red. Bull Beef is of a closer grain, and a deep dusk red, and has a rankish smell; and the fat skinny and hard.

N. B. Observe right Ox Beef when a round is cut off the Leg, it appears so juicy as if it was full of gravy.

To chuse Pork.

For roasting buy small Pig Pork, the lean must be near as fine as veal in the grain; the fat firm and of a fine white colour. If the lean be reddish and the fat yellow, it is tainted, or has not been properly attended to in the feeding. For boiling, let your Pork be fatter than roasting, and of a fine grain.

To chuse Brawn.

Thick Brawn is old, the moderate is young. If the rind and fat be very tender, it is not boar-brawn, but barrow or sow.

To chuse Hams.

Put a knife under the bone that sticks out of the Ham, and if it comes out clean, and has a good flavour, it is sweet and good; if much smeared and dull, it is tainted and rusty.

To chuse Bacon.

If the fat be white, oily in feeling, and does not break or crumble, and the flesh sticks well to the bones,

and

and bears a good colour it is good; but if the contrary, and the lean has some little streaks of yellow, it is rusty or will soon be so.

To chuse Butter.

When you buy Butter, trust not to that which will be given you to taste, but try in the middle, and if your smell and taste be good, you cannot be deceived.

To chuse Cheese.

Cheese is to be chosen by its moist and smooth coat; if old cheese be rough-coated, rugged or dry at top, beware of little worms or mites. If it be all over full of holes, moist or spungy, it is subject to maggot. If any soft or perished place appear on the outside, try how deep it goes, for the greater part may be hid within.

To chuse Eggs.

Hold the great end to your tongue, if it feels warm it is new, if cold it is bad; and so on in proportion to the heat and cold so is the goodness of the Egg. Another way to know a good Egg is, to put the Egg into a pan of cold water, the fresher it is, the sooner it will fall to the bottom; if rotten it will not sink at all.

To keep Eggs good.

Place them all with the small end downwards in fine wood ashes, turning them once a week end ways, and they will keep some months.

To chuse Poultry.

A Cock or Capon, &c. If they are young, their spurs are short and dubbed; but take particular notice they are not pared or scraped. If the hen is old her legs and comb are rough; if young, smooth.

A Turkey. If the cock be young, his legs will be black and smooth, and his spurs short; if stale, his eyes will be sunk in his head, and his feet dry; if new, the eyes lively and limber. For the hen observe the same directions; and if she is with egg, she will have a soft open vent; if not, a hard close one.

A Goose. If the bill is yellowish, and has but few hairs, it is young; but if full of hairs, and the bill and foot red, it is old; if fresh, limber footed; if stale, dry footed.

Ducks, wild or tame. If fresh, limber footed; if stale, dry footed.

A true wild duck has a reddish foot, and smaller than the tame one.

To chuse a Rabbit or Coney.

If a Rabbit be old, the claws will be very long and rough, and grey hairs intermixed with the wool; but if young, the claws and wool smooth; if stale it will be limber, and the flesh will look blueish, having a kind of slime upon it; but if fresh, it will be stiff, and the flesh white and dry.

To chuse Pigeons, &c.

The Dove-house Pigeons when old, are red-legged; when new and fat, limber footed and feel full in the vent; when stale their vents are green and flabby.

To chuse Fish.

Salmon, Whiting, Pike, Trout, Carp, Tench, Grayling, Barbel, Chub, Ruff, Eel, Smelt, Shad, &c. All these are known to be new or stale by the colour of their gills; their easiness or hardness to open, the hanging or keeping up their fins, the standing out or sinking of their eyes, &c. &c. or by smelling their gills.

Turbot. He is chosen by his thickness and plumpness; and if his belly be of a cream colour, he must spend well; but if thin, and his belly of a blueish white, he will eat very loose.

Cod and Codling. Chuse them by their thickness towards the head, and the whiteness of the flesh when it is cut.

Ling. For dried Ling, chuse that which is thickest in the poll, and the flesh of the brightest yellow.

Scate and Thornback. Chuse them by their thickness; and the She-skate is always the sweetest, especially if large.

Soals. These are chosen by their thickness and stiffness; when their bellies are of a cream colour, they spend the firmer.

Sturgeon. If it cuts without crumbling, and the veins and gristle give a true blue where they appear, and the flesh a perfect white, then conclude it to be good.

Mackarel.

Mackarel and fresh Herrings. If the gills are of a lively and shining redness, their eyes stand full and the flesh is stiff, then they are new; but if dusky and faded, or sinking and wrinkled, and the tails limber, they are stale.

Flounders and Plaice. If they are stiff, and their eyes be not sunk or look dull, they are new; the contrary when stale. The best of Plaice look blueish on the belly.

Lobsters. Chuse them by their weight, the heaviest are the best, if no water is in them; if new, the tail will fly up like a spring; if full, the middle of the tail will be of hard, reddish, skinned meat.

Prawns, Shrimps, and Crab-fish. The two first, if stale, will cast a kind of slimy smell, their colour fading, and they slimy; otherwise all of them are good.—The latter, if stale will be limber in their claws and joints, their red colour turned blackish and dusky, and will have an ill smell under their throats.

Pickled Salmon. If the flesh feels oily, the scales stiff and shining, and it comes in flakes, and parts without crumbling, then it is new and good, and not otherwise.

Poultry in Season.

January. Hen Turkeys, Capons, Pullets with eggs, Fowls, Chickens, Hares, all sorts of wild Fowl, tame Rabbits and tame Pigeons.

February. Turkeys, &c. as above, in this month begin to decline, Green Geese, young Ducklings, and Turkey Poults.

March. This month the same as the preceding months; only wild fowl goes quite out.

April. Pullets, spring Fowls, Chickens, Pigeons, young Wild Rabbits, Leverets, young Geese, Ducklings, and Turkey Poults.

May and *June* the same.

July. The same, with young Partridges, Pheasants, and Wild Ducks, called Flappers or Moulters.

August the same.

September, October, November, and *December.* In these months all sorts of fowls, both wild and tame, are in season; and the three last, is the full season for all manner of wild fowl.

Fish in Season.

January. Salmon, Cod, Turbit, Soles, Carp, Tench, Eels, Lamperys, Flounders, Plaice, Whitings, Thorback, Skate, Smelts, Sturgeon, Cray-fish, Haddock, Crabs, Lobsters, Prawns, and Oysters.

February. Turbit, Cod, Salmon, Soles, Whitings, Haddocks, Sturgeon, Skate, Plaice, Flounders, Smelts, Tench, Carp, Lampray, Eels, Crabs, Lobsters, Oysters, Prawns, Cray-fish.

March. Salmon, Ling, Skate, Soles, Whitings, Turbit, Flounders, Carp, Tench, Lobster, Crabs, Cray-fish, Prawns, and Oysters.

April. Salmon, Ling, Carp, Tench, Turbit, Trouts, Skate, Smelts, Prawns, Lobsters, and Crabs.

May. Salmon, Trout, Soles, Carp, Tench, Eels, Herrings, Smelts, Turbit, Lobster, Cray-fish, Crabs, and Prawns.

June. Gilts, Trout, Pike, Eels, Soles, Turbit, Carp, Tench, Mackarel, Herrings, Smelts, Lobsters, Cray-fish, Shrimps, Lamprays, and Prawns.

July. Turbit, Gilts, Cod, Mackarel, Herrings, Soles, Skate, Flounders, Plaice, Pike, Carp, Tench, Eels, Lobsters, Prawns, Cray-fish, and Shrimps.

August. Pike, Cod, Flounders, Plaice, Skate, Thornback, Mackarels, Herrings, Carp, Eels, Cray-fish, Prawns, Oysters, and Lobsters.

September. Cod, Soles, Skate, Flounders, Plaice, Smelts, Pike, Carp, Tench, Lobsters, and Oysters.

October. Pike, Carp, Tench, Smelts, John Dorees, Soles, Perch, Brills, Codlins, Oysters.

November. Dorees, Smelts, Barbets, Gurnets, Carp, Pike, Tench, Whitings, Haddocks, Codlings, Oysters, Cockles, Shrimps, Soles, Turbit, & Lobsters.

December. Turbit, Sturgeon, Salmon, Dorees, Smelts, Cod, Codlings, Haddocks, Soles, Carp, Tench, Oysters, Crabs, Lobsters, Prawns, & Cray-fish.

Directions *for* ROASTING *all Manner of* Butcher's Meat, &c.

General Directions.

IF you are to roast any thing very small or thin, take care to have a pretty little brisk fire, that it may be done quick and nice; if a large joint, such as a haunch of venison, or a piece of beef, be sure to make on a good fire, let it be clear at the bottom, and keep your meat at a distance, that it may roast gradually, and not scorch. Before you send it to table, take off your paper, and froth it up; for which purpose tie it round with buttered paper and twine; but no skewers for fear of letting out the gravy, keeping basting it with the dripping. When you roast a hare or a rabbit, take care that the ends are well done; when they are half roasted, cut the neck-skin to let out the blood, or it will mix with the sauce when they are cut up, and be very disagreeable.—When you hash or mince any kind of meat or fowl, do not make the gravy too thick. It should be no thicker than thin cream, or melted butter.—Take great care the spit be very clean, and be sure to clean it with nothing but sand and water. Wash it clean and wipe it with a dry cloth, for oil, brick-dust, and all such things will be very offensive.

N. B. In frosty weather meat in general takes more roasting than at other times.

Directions for Poultry:—Let your fire be very quick and clear when you lay your poultry down to roast, otherwise it will not eat near so sweet, or look so beautiful to the eye.

Times of roasting:—A middling turkey or goose will take an hour; a very large one an hour and a quarter. A large fowl or tame duck, three quarters of an hour; a middling one half an hour; very small ones twenty minutes. Wild ducks, teal, wigeon, &c. ten minutes; but if you love them well done, a quarter of an hour. Woodcocks, snipes and partridges, twenty; pigeons, larks, &c. fifteen minutes.

To roast Beef.

Observe the General Directions as to large and small joints of Beef: and when you see the smoke draws to the fire, it will be near enough.

N. B. As some chuse their Beef unsalted but at the fire, rub it well with a dry cloth, and dip the cloth in vinegar, and that will prevent the flies hurting it, and make it keep. When at the fire, after basting it, salt it according to your taste.

To roast Lamb or Mutton.

For large joints of Mutton, observe the same directions as for Beef, the salt excepted. When you roast the saddle or loin of Mutton, besure to skin it, and tie it on with a little twine, that your gravy be preserved, and your Mutton is not too brown.

To roast Veal.

Stuffing for a fillet, or any other joint of Veal: Grated bread, and as much suet as bread, a little sweet marjoram, parsley, mace, nutmeg, salt, mixed with two eggs, and as much cream as will drach it into a paste; which put under the udder, or the kell of the fillet.

N. B. If a shoulder, some chuse to baste it with cream till half done, then flour it, and baste it with butter.

The breast may be roasted with the caul on 'till it is enough, and the sweetbread skewered on the backside of the breast. When it is near enough, take off the caul, baste it and dredge it with flour. All these are to be sent to table with melted butter and garnished with sliced lemon.

If a loin or fillet not stuffed, be sure to paper the fat, that as little may be lost as possible. All joints are to be laid at a diſtance from the fire, 'till ſoaked, then near the fire. When you lay it down, baſte it with good butter; (except it be the ſhoulder, and that may be done the ſame if you rather chuſe it) and when it is near enough, baſte it again, and dredge it with a very little flour.

To roaſt a Pig.

Before you ſpit it, and after it is laid down to the fire, and thoroughly dried, dip a cloth in a little ſweet oil, and keep conſtantly rubbing with it till enough, to prevent it from bliſtering. And when done, cut off the head, and ſplit it through the back before you draw the ſpit out. Cut off the ears, place one on each ſhoulder, and the jaw bone on each ſide the diſh. Serve it up with your ſauce, mixed with a little of the ſage and the bread within it, as well as the brains. —Make the ſauce thus: Take the brains of the Pig, chop them a little, put them into a ſauce-pan with a little gravy, add five ounces of butter, a little flour, pepper, and ſalt, ſtir it over the fire 'till it boils, then pour it into your diſh under your Pig, and give your diſh a ſhake to mix the ſauce with the ſage and parſley that were in the Pig.

To roaſt Pork.

The beſt way to roaſt a leg is to ſtuff it with a little ſage ſhred fine, a little pepper and ſalt, and onion, if you like it; and when roaſting and near done, ſtrew ſome crumbs of bread and ſhred parſley over it; then have a little drawn gravy to put in the diſh with the crumbs that drop from it. Some like the knuckle ſtuffed with onions, and
ſage

sage shred small, with a little pepper and salt, gravy and apple-sauce to it; this they call a *mock goose*: The spring or hand of pork, if very young, roasted like a pig eats very well, otherwise it is best boiled: The spare-rib should be basted with a little bit of butter, a very little flour and some sage shred small, and served up with apple-sauce. The best way to dress pork griskins is to roast them, baste them with butter and crumbs of bread, sage, and a little pepper and salt. The sauce to these is mustard.

When you roast a loin, take a sharp penknife and cut the skin across to make the crackling eat the better. If pork is not well done, it is apt to surfeit.

To roast a hind quarter of Pig, Lamb-fashion.

At the time of year when house-lamb is very dear, take the hind-quarter of a large pig, take off the skin, and roast it, and it will eat like lamb, with mint sauce or with a sallad, or Seville oranges.

To roast Mutton like Venison.

Take a fat hind quarter of Mutton, and cut the leg like a haunch of Venison, rub it well with salt petre, hang it in a moist part for two days, wiping it two or three times a day with a clean cloth, then put it into a pan, and having boiled a quarter of an ounce of all-spice in a quart of red wine, pour it boiling hot over your mutton, and cover it close for two hours, then take it out, spit it, lay it to the fire, and constantly baste it with some liquor and butter. If you have a good quick fire, and your mutton not very large, it will be ready in an hour and a half;

half; then take it up, and send it to table, with some good gravy in one cup, and Venison sauce in another.

To roast a Hare.

Case it, leave on the ears, and wipe it clean in the inside; double the hind legs and skewer them, lay the fore ones close to the side, and skewer them also; turn the head back, and skewer it; put a skewer into each ear to keep them up; then spit it. One side being larded, and not the other, and while it is roasting, baste it with milk or cream, then serve it up with Venison sauce.

Another way.

Take some liver of a hare, some fat bacon, grated bread, an anchovy, shalot, a little winter-savoury and some nutmeg; beat all these into a paste, and put them into the belly of the Hare; baste the Hare with stale beer, put a little bit of bacon in the pan, when it is half roasted baste it with the butter. For sauce, take melted butter and some winter savoury.

Another way.

Set and lard it with bacon, make for it a pudding of grated bread, the heart and liver parboiled and chopped small with beef suet and sweet herbs mixt with marrow, cream, spice and eggs, then sew up the belly and roast it. When it is roasted let your butter be drawn up with cream, gravy, or red wine.

To roast Rabbits.

Skewer the legs as a hare, or tuck the fore legs into the body; skewer them together, and put the spit between them, let their heads be streight out, and nick them in the neck, that the blood may run out when roasting. Lay them down to a moderate fire, dust with flour and baste them with good butter, and having boiled the liver with a bunch of parsley, and chopped them small, put half into the butter, pour it into the dish, and garnish it with the other half.

To roast a Rabbit Hare fashion.

Lard a Rabbit with bacon; roast it as you do a Hare, and it eats very well. But then you must make gravy-sauce; but if you do not lard it, white-sauce.

To roast a Haunch of Venison.

Take a Haunch of Venison and spit it, then take some wheat flour and water, knead and roll it very thin, tie it over the fat part of the Venison with pack-thread; if it be a large haunch it will take four hours roasting, and a middling haunch three hours; keep basting all the time you roast it. When you dish it up, put a little gravy in the dish, and sweet sauce in a bason; half an hour before you draw your Venison take off the paste, baste it and let it be a light brown.

To roast a Neat's Tongue.

Take a pickled Tongue and boil it 'till the skin will come off, and when it is skinned, stick it with cloves about two inches asunder, then put it on a spit and wrap a veal caul over it, and roast it 'till it is enough; then take off the caul and just froth it up, and serve it in a dish with gravy, and some venison or claret sauce on a plate; garnish it with raspings of bread sifted and lemon sliced.

To roast a Tongue or Udder.

Parboil your Tongue or Udder, then stick into it ten or twelve cloves, and whilst it is roasting baste it with butter. When it is ready take it up, and send it to table with some gravy in the dish and sweet-sauce in a boat.

To roast a Breast of Mutton.

Bone the Mutton, make a savoury-forced meat for it, wash it over with the batter of eggs, then spread the forced meat on it; roll it on a collar, and bind it with a pack-thread; then roast it, put under it a regalia of cucumbers.

To roast a Chine of Pork.

Take a chine of pork, sprinkle it with a little salt, and hang it up for two days; then spit it, score it just through the skin, leaving half an inch between every score, and lay it down to roast for two hours; or more, if it is a large one. Let the skin be of a nice brown, and crisp, taking care you do not scorch it; serve it up hot with some gravy under it, and apple sauce in a boat.

To roast a Chine of Pork with Stuffing.

Make a stuffing of the fat leaf of pork, parsley, sage, eggs, crumbs of bread, season it with pepper, salt, shalot, and nutmeg, and stuff it thick; then roast it gently, and when it is quarter-roasted cut the skin in slips, and make your sauce with apples, lemon-peel, two or three cloves, and a blade of mace, and have mustard in a cup.

To roast Larks.

Take a dozen of larks, let them be clean pick'd, cut off their heads, turn their feet back, put them on a long skewer, tie them on a spit, dust and baste them; have ready a good many crumbs of bread in a dish, hold the dish with the crumbs under your larks, and strew the larks with them, then baste them with butter, and continue so doing 'till your larks are quite covered with crumbs, and of a nice brown;—take care when you dish them up, that you do not shake the crumbs of bread off; if you do, it will spoil the look of them; let the crumbs be continued under the larks till brown, and put them round the dish. Serve them up hot for a second course, or for supper, with plain melted butter in a boat.

To roast Woodcocks.

When you have trussed your Woodcocks, and drawn them under the leg, whilst the Woodcock is roasting baste it with butter, set it under an earthen dish with a slice of toasted bread in it, and let the Woodcock drop upon it; your Woodcock will take about 20 minutes roasting if you have a good fire. When you dish it up, lay the toast under it, and serve it up with gravy.

To roast Snipes.

Spit them on a small bird-spit, flour them and baste them with butter, then have ready a slice of bread toasted brown, lay it in a dish, and set it under the Snipes for the trail to drop on; they will take about 15 minutes; and when enough, lay them on the toast; have ready for two Snipes, a quarter of a pint of good beef gravy hot, pour it into the dish, and set it over a chaffing-dish two or three minutes, and send them hot to table. Woodcocks may be done in the same way.

To roaſt Partridges or Quails.

Pick them, draw and ſkewer them with their legs on; ſpit, ſinge, and baſte them; they will take 20 minutes at a quick fire; dredge them with flour, and baſte them with butter, let them be of a nice brown, diſh them up with ſome brown gravy under them, and ſome bread ſauce in a boat, for a 2d courſe, or ſupper diſh.

To dreſs a Wild Duck the beſt way.

Firſt half roaſt it, then lay it in a diſh, carve it, but leave the joints hanging together, throw a little pepper and ſalt, and ſqueeze the juice of a lemon over it, turn it on the breaſt, and preſs hard with a plate, and add to its own gravy, two or three ſpoonfuls of good gravy, cover it cloſe with another diſh, and ſet over a ſtove ten minutes, then it muſt be carried to table hot in the diſh it was done in, and garniſh'd with lemon. You may add a little red wine, and a ſhalot cut ſmall, if you like it, but it is apt to make the Duck eat hard, unleſs you firſt heat the wine and pour it in juſt as it is done.

To roaſt a Gooſe.

Take ſage, waſh it, pick it clean, chop it ſmall, with pepper and ſalt; roll them with butter, and put them into the belly; never put onion into any thing, unleſs you are ſure every body loves it; take care that your Gooſe be clean picked and drawn; and then you are ſure it is clean. If a young gooſe, you may ſcald it; roaſt it and baſte it with butter, and when it is half done throw ſome flour over it, that it may have a fine brown. Three quarters of an hour will do it at a quick fire if it is not too large, otherwife it will require an hour. Always have good gravy in a bafon, and apple-fauce in another.

When you roaft a goofe, turkey, or fowls of any fort, take care to finge them with a piece of white paper, and bafte them with a piece of butter; dredge them with a little flour, and when the fmoke begins to draw to the fire, and they look plump, bafte them again, and dredge them with a little flour, and fend them to table.

A Green Goofe.

Never put any feafoning into it, unlefs defired. You muft either put good gravy, or green-fauce (with goofe-berries) in the difh, made thus: take a handful of forrel, beat it in a mortar, and fqueeze the juice out, add to it a little fugar and melted butter. Or made thus: take half a pint of the juice of forrel, a fpoonful of white wine, a little grated nutmeg, a little grated bread; boil thefe a quarter of an hour foftly, then ftrain it, and put it into the fauce-pan again, and fweeten it with a little fugar, give it a boil and pour it into a difh or bafon; fome like a little piece of butter rolled in flour, and put into it.

To roaft a Turkey.

Take a quarter of a pound of lean veal, fome parfley, fweet marjoram, a bit of lemon-peel, a fmall bit of onion, a little nutmeg grated, a little mace, fome falt and fuet; cut your herbs very fmall, pound your meat as fmall as poffible, and mix all together with three eggs, and as much bread as will make it of a proper confiftence; then fill the crop of your turkey with it, paper the

the breaſt, and lay it down at a good diſtance from the fire. When the ſmoke begins to draw to the fire and it looks plump, baſte it again, and dredge it with ſome flour, then take it up and ſend it to table.—If no veal, make your forcement of two parts ſuet and one bread —A large turkey generally takes an hour and a quarter; and a middle-ſized one three quarters of an hour.

Sauce for a roaſted Turkey.

For the Sauce, take ſome white gravy, catch-up, a few bread crumbs and ſome whole pepper; let them boil well together, put to them ſome flour and a lump of butter, which pour upon the turkey. You may lay round your turkey forced meat balls. Garniſh your diſh with lemon.

To roaſt a Fowl or Turkey with Cheſnuts.

Take a quarter of a hundred cheſnuts, roaſt and peel them; bruiſe about a dozen of them in a mortar, with the liver of the fowl, a quarter of a pound of ham, and ſome ſweet herbs; mix theſe together with ſome mace, pepper, ſalt, and nutmeg, and having put them into your fowl, ſpit and roaſt it, and baſte it with butter. For ſauce, take the reſt of the cheſnuts, chop them ſmall, and put them into ſome ſtrong gravy, with a glaſs of white wine, and a piece of butter rolled in flour: pour the ſauce in the diſh, and garniſh with water-creſſes and ſliced orange.

To roaſt a Turkey Pout.

Take a young turkey, rather larger than a half-grown fowl, ſcald and draw it clean, ſkewer it with its head down to its ſides, ſpit it, and lay it down to a clear fire for 20 minutes; baſte it it well with butter, and duft it with flour, let it be plump, and of a nice brown, lay it in a difh, with fome brown gravy under it, and ferve it up hot for a fecond courfe, with fome bread fauce in a boat.

To roaft a Capon.

Pick it clean, draw it, and finge it then or upon the fpit; cut the feet off, and fkewer the legs ftreight, fo fpit it; duft and bafte it. When ready, difh it with fome thick gravy, and lay parts of a lemon round the difh; and with a boat of egg fauce. It will take near an hour.

To roaft Pheafants or Moor Game.

Pick and draw your pheafants, (or moor game) and finge them, lard one with bacon, but not the other, fpit them, roaft them fine, and paper them all over the breaft, when they are juft done, flour and bafte them with a little nice butter, and let them have a fine white froth; then take them up, and pour good gravy in the difh and bread fauce in a boat—At a good fire half an hour will do them.

To roaft a Fowl pheafant fafhion.

If you fhould have but one pheafant, and want two in a difh, take a large full-grown fowl, keep the head on, and trufs it juft as you do a pheafant, lard it with bacon; but don't lard the pheafant, and nobody will know it.

To roaft Pigeons.

Stuff them with a piece of butter, fome chopped parfley, pepper, falt, and the liver fhred fmall; fkewer them with their legs on the breaft, breaſt, then put them on a ſmall ſpit, flour them, and baſte them with butter: they will be done in fifteen or twenty minutes. Many people roaſt them by a ſtring faſtened to the top of the chimney-piece. When they are enough, lay them in the diſh, and put bunches of aſparagus round them, with parſley and butter for ſauce.

To make muſhroom ſauce for white fowls of all ſorts.

Take a pint of muſhrooms, waſh and pick them very clean, put them into a ſauce-pan, with a little ſalt, ſome nutmeg, a blade of mace, a pint of cream, and a good piece of butter rolled in flour; boil theſe all together, and keep ſtirring them, then pour your ſauce in the diſh and garniſh with lemon.

To make celery-ſauce either for roaſted or boiled fowls, Turkies, Partridges, or any other game.

Take a large bunch of celery, waſh and pare it very clean, cut it in thin bits, and boil it ſoftly in a little water till it is tender; then add a little beaten mace, nutmeg, pepper and ſalt, thicken'd with a good piece of butter rolled in flour, boil it up, and then pour it in your diſh.

A good ſauce for Teal, Mallard, Ducks, &c.

Take a quantity of veal gravy, according to the bigneſs of your diſh of wild fowl, ſeaſoned with pepper and ſalt; ſqueeze in the juice of two oranges and ſome red wine. This will ſerve all ſorts of wild fowl.

General

General Directions *for* Boiling Meat.

ALL fresh meat should be put into the water boiling hot, and salt meat when the water is cold, unless you apprehend it is not corn'd quite enough; and in that case putting it into the water when hot strikes in the salt

Chickens, lamb, veal, and pork are much whiter for being boiled in a clean linen cloth with a little milk and flour in your water.

Observe that the time sufficient for dressing different joints depends on the size. A leg of mutton, of about seven or eight pounds, will take two hours boiling A young fowl about half an hour. A middle-sized leg of lamb about an hour and a quarter. A thick piece of beef, of twelve or fourteen pounds, will take about two hours and a half after the water boils, if you put in the beef when the water is cold; and so in proportion to the thickness and weight of the piece; but all kinds of victuals take somewhat more time in frosty weather. Upon the whole, the best rule to be observed is, to allow a quarter of an hour to every pound, when the joint is put into boiling water.

N. B. In case the cook should neglect to skim the pot when it boils, the scum will boil down and settle upon your meat, and make it black; and always keep your pot very clean.

To keep Meat hot.

Set the dish over a pan of boiling water, cover it with a deep cover so as not to touch the meat, and lay a cloth over all: This way will keep your meat hot a long time, and it is better than over-roasting and spoiling the meat. The steam of the water keeps the meat hot, and does not draw the gravy out, or dry it up; whereas if you set a dish of meat over a chaffing-dish of coals, it will dry up the gravy, and spoil the meat. *For*

For boiling a Leg of Lamb, with the Loin fried about it.

Take a leg of house-lamb of 4 lb. weight, break the shank off, and pare it neatly round, leaving out a little of the shank bone; nick it in joint, rub it over with a little butter, and dust it with flour, wrap it in a cloth, (as all white meat must be) boil it and lay it in the dish, then pour a little parsley and butter over it, and lay your fried lamb round it; cut some asparagus the size of pease, boil it green, and lay it round your lamb in spoonfuls, and garnish the dish with crisp'd parsley; or serve it with spinage or colliflowers.

A Leg of Lamb boiled with Chickens round it.

When your Lamb is boiled, pour over it parsley and butter; lay your chickens round it, and pour over them a little white fricasey sauce; garnish you dish with sippets and lemons.

To boil a Ham.

Before you boil a ham, let it be steeped in warm water for two nights and a day; tie it up in cloth, and put it into a pot of cold hard water, to which add a little new hay. Let it boil gently for three or four hours, and keep it well skimmed all the time; if it is a small one, an hour and a half boiling will do it; then take off the rind, and sprinkle it over with raspings of bread, and a little shred parsley; then set it before the fire to crisp.—Many people approve of a baked ham to a boiled one; the best method is to steep it in cold water a day or two, according to its size and dryness, previous to baking; then take

take it out, wash it clean, and dry it well with a cloth. Then make a thick paste with common houshold bread, as much as will roll it quite round, then put into a pot and send it to the bake-house; when done, take the paste clean off, and send it hot to table.

To boil a Tongue.

Lay a dried tongue in cold water all night; when you put it in to boil, put in cold water, and let it boil three hours, or to its size. If it be just out of pickle, it must lay three hours in cold water, and then boiled till it will peel.

To boil pickled Pork.

Be sure to put it in when the water boils. If a middling piece an hour will boil it; if a very large piece an hour and a half, or two hours. If you boil pickled pork too long it will go to a jelly.

To boil Rabbits.

Truss them for boiling, and lard them with bacon; then boil them quick and white. For sauce, take the boiled liver and shred it with fat bacon; toss these up together in some gravy, white wine vinegar, nutmeg, mace and salt; set parsley, minced barberries, and drawn butter: Lay your rabbits in a dish, and pour the sauce over them. Garnish it with sliced lemon and barberries.

To boil Rabbits and Onion Sauce.

Truss your rabbits, tuck in the fore legs, and skewer up the head, skewer the hind legs close to the sides; rub them over with butter, dust them with flour, and tie them up in a clean cloth; if they are young, half an hour will do;
if

if larger, three quarters of an hour. When diſhed, pour onion ſauce over them.

To boil Pigeons.

Boil them by themſelves for fifteen minutes, then boil a handſome ſquare piece of bacon and lay in the middle; ſtew ſome ſpinage to lay round, and lay the pigeons on it. Garniſh your diſh with parſley laid in a plate before the fire to criſp. Or lay one pigeon in the middle and the reſt round, and the ſpinage between each pigeon, and a ſlice of bacon on each pigeon. Garniſh with ſlices of bacon and melted butter in a cup.

To boil a Pheaſant.

Take a fine pheaſant, boil it in a good deal of water, keep your water boiling; half an hour will do a ſmall one, and an hour a large one. Let your ſauce be celery ſtewed and thickened with cream, and a little butter rolled in flour; take up the pheaſant and pour the ſauce all over it. Garniſh with lemon.

To boil Chickens.

Take four or five chickens, as you would have your diſh in bigneſs; if they be ſmall ſcald them, then pluck them, which will make them whiter; then draw them, and take out the breaſt-bone, waſh and truſs them, cut off the heads and necks, tie them in a napkin, and boil them in milk (mixed with a little flour, which hinders the milk from curdling) and water about 20 or 25 minutes. They are better for being killed the night before you uſe them. If large fowls, they are ſerved up in the ſame manner, but take longer boiling. *For*

For making sauce to the Chickens.

Boil the necks, livers and gizzards in water, when they are enough strain off the gravy, and put a spoonful of oyster-pickle to it, break the livers small, mix a little gravy, and rub them through a hair-sieve with the back of a spoon; then put a spoonful of cream to it, a little lemon and lemon-peel grated, thicken it with butter and flour. Let your sauce be no thicker than cream, pour it upon your chickens. Garnish the dish with sippets, mushrooms and slices of lemons.

To boil Ducks with onion sauce.

Take two fat ducks, season them with a little pepper and salt, skewer them up at both ends, and boil them whilst they are tender; take four or five large onions, boil them in milk and water, change the water two or three times in the boiling; when they are enough chop them very small, and rub them through a hair-sieve with the back of a spoon, then melt a little butter, put in your onions and a little salt, and pour it upon your ducks. Garnish with onions and sippets.

To boil a Turkey.

Draw and truss your turkey, cut off the feet, and cut down the breast-bone with a knife; then sew up the skin again, and stuff the breast with the following stuffing.

Boil a sweet-bread of veal, chop it fine with a little lemon-peel, a handful of bread crumbs, a little beef-suet, part of the liver, a spoonful or two of cream, with pepper, salt, nutmeg, and two eggs; mix all together, and stuff your turkey

key with part of the stuffing, the rest may be fried or boiled, to lay round it; dredge it with a little flour, tie it up in a cloth, and boil it with milk and water; an hour will do for a large, and three-quarters for a middle sized one.

Sauce for a boiled Turkey.

Take a pint of oysters, two or three spoonfuls of cream, a little juice of lemon, a little small white gravy, and salt to your taste; thicken it with flour and butter, then pour it over your turkey, and serve it up; lay round the turkey fried oysters and forced meat. Garnish the dish with mushrooms, oysters, and slices of lemon.

Mushroom-sauce for white Fowls boiled.

Take half a pint of cream, and a quarter of a pound of butter, stir them together one way till it is thick; then add a spoonful of mushroom pickle, pickled mushrooms, or fresh if you have them. Garnish only with lemon.

Directions for boiling GREENS, ROOTS, &c.

ALWAYS be very careful that your greens be nicely picked and washed. You should lay them in a clean pan, for fear of sand or dust, which is apt to hang round wooden vessels. Boil all your greens in a copper sauce-pan, well tinned, by themselves, with a great deal of water. Boil no meat with them, for that discolours them. Use no iron pans, &c. for they are not proper.

To dress Spinage.

Pick it very clean, and wash it in five or six waters; put it in a sauce pan, with a little butter at the bottom, that will just hold it, throw a little salt over it, and cover the pan close. Do not put any water in, but shake the pan often. You must put your sauce-pan on a clear quick fire. As soon as you find the greens are shrunk and fallen to the bottom, and that the liquor which comes out of them boils up, they are enough. Throw them into a clean sieve to drain, and give them a little squeeze. Lay them in a plate, and never put any butter on, but put it in a cup.

To dress Cabbages, &c.

Cabbage, and all sorts of young sprouts, must be boiled in a great deal of water. When the stalks are tender, or fallen to the bottom, they are enough; then take them off, before they lose their colour. Always throw salt in your water before you put your greens in. Young sprouts you send to table just as they are, but cabbage is best squeezed between two trenchers.

To dress Carrots.

Let them be scraped very clean, and when they are enough rub them in a clean cloth, then slice them into a plate, and pour some melted butter over them. If they are young spring carrots, half an hour will boil them; if large, an hour; but old carrots will take two hours.

To dress Turnips.

They eat best boiled in the pot, and when enough take them out and put them in a pan and

and mash them with butter and salt, and send them to table. But you may do them thus: Pare your turnips, and cut them into dice, as big as the top of one's finger; put them in a clean sauce-pan, and just cover them with water. When enough, throw them into a sieve to drain, and put them into a sauce-pan with a good piece of butter; stir them over the fire for five or six minutes, and send them to table.

To dress Parsnips.

Boil them in a deal of water, and when you find they are soft take them up, scrape all the dirt off them, and with a knife scrape them fine, throwing away all the sticky parts; then put them into a sauce-pan, with some milk, and stir them over the fire till they are thick; take great care they don't burn, add a good piece of butter and a little salt, and when the butter is melted send them to table.

To dress Brockala.

Strip off all the branches till you come to the top one, then with a knife peel off the hard outside skin, which is on the stalks and little branches, and tie them up as asparagus, and throw them into water; have a stew-pan of water with some salt in it, when it boils put in the brockala, and when the stalks are tender it is enough, then send it to table with butter in a cup.

To dress Potatoes.

Boil them in as little water as you can, cover the sauce-pan close, and when the skin cracks they are enough; drain all the water out, and let them stand covered for a minute or two, then peel them, and have ready boiled milk and water to throw them into, as you pare them, which will keep them hot and of a good colour, till you fend them to table, but drain them through a cullender.

To drefs Cauliflowers.

Take off all the green part, cut the flowers into four quarters, and lay them in water for an hour; then put them into fome boiling milk and water, and be fure to fkim the fauce pan well; when the ftalks are tender, take them carefully up, and put them in a cullender to drain; then difh them, and ferve them with melted butter.

To drefs French Beans.

String them, cut them in two, and afterwards acrofs; lay them into water and falt, and when the pan boils put in fome falt and the beans; when they are tender they are enough; they will be foon done. Take care they don't lofe their fine green. Lay them on a plate, and ferve them with butter in a cup.

To drefs Beans and Bacon.

Boil the bacon by itfelf, and the beans by themfelves, for the bacon will fpoil the colour of the beans; always throw fome falt into the water, and fome parfley nicely picked; when the bacon is enough, take it up and fkin it, throw fome rafpings of bread over the top, and fet it before the fire to brown. Send them to table with butter in a bafon.

To drefs Artichokes.

Wring off the ftalks, and put them into the water

water cold with the tops downwards, that all the dust and sand may boil out. When the water boils, an hour and a half will do them.

To dress Asparagus.

Scrape all the stalks very carefully till they look white, then cut all the stalks even alike, throw them into water, and have ready a stew-pan boiling. Put in some salt, and tie the asparagus in little bundles. Let the water keep boiling, and when they are a little tender take them up. If you boil them too much you lose both colour and taste. Cut the round of a small loaf about half an inch thick, toast it brown on both sides, dip it in the asparagus liquor, and lay it in your dish: pour a little butter over the toast, then lay your asparagus on the toast all round the dish, with the white tops outward. Don't pour butter over the asparagus, for that makes them greasy to the fingers, but have your butter in a bason, and send it to table.

Concerning boiling Greens, &c.

Most people spoil garden things by over-boiling them. All things that are green should have a little crispness, for if they are over-boiled they neither have any sweetness or beauty.

HASHING, STEWING, BAKING, &c.

HASHING.—*To hash a Calf's Head.*

HALF boil it, cut it in small slices, season it with salt, nutmeg and mace; put in a bunch

bunch of sweet herbs, an onion stuck with cloves; all which put into your gravy, and let it stew very slowly; thicken it with the yolk of an egg and a little of the gravy, with a few spoonfuls of white wine.—Take care the yolk of your egg don't break.

Another.

After slicing it as before, take some strong gravy, a gill of red wine, a few sweet-breads, a little lemon-peel, and some spice; toss it up with a little butter, and take it to table.

To hash Beef.

Cut some tender beef in slices, put it into a stew-pan well floured, with a slice of butter, over a quick fire, for three minutes, and then add a little water, a bunch of sweet herbs, some lemon-peel, an onion, or a little marjoram, with pepper, salt, and grated nutmeg; cover it close and let it stew till it is tender; then put in a glass of red wine or strong beer, strain your sauce, serve it hot, and garnish with lemon and beet root.

To hash a Leg of Mutton.

Half roast your mutton, and when it is cold cut it into thin pieces, put it into a stew-pan with a little water or small gravy, two or three spoonfuls of red wine, two or three onions, and three spoonfuls of oyster pickle; thicken it with flour, and serve it up. Garnish the dish with horse-radish and pickle.

You may do a shoulder of mutton the same way, only boil the blade-bone, and lay it in the middle.

To hash any part of Mutton.

Cut the mutton into small pieces, then take about half a pint of oysters, after washing them in water, put them into their own liquor in a sauce-pan, with some whole pepper, mace, and a little salt; when it is stewed a little put in a spoonful of catchup, an anchovy or pickled walnut liquor, some gravy or water; then put in your mutton, and a piece of butter rolled in flour; let it boil till the mutton is warm through, then add a glass of red wine, lay it upon sippets, garnish with sliced lemon or capers, and mushrooms.

To hash any sort of Meat.

Take a little whole pepper, salt, a few sprigs of sweet herbs, a little anchovy, one shalot, two slices of lemon, let it stew a little, and thicken it with burnt butter. When you have no gravy, boil the bones of your meat for to make the gravy. Serve it with pickles and sippets.

STEWING.
How to stew a rump of Beef.

Take a fat rump of beef, cut off the fag end, lard the lower part with fat bacon, and stuff the other part with shred parsley, put into your pan as much water as will cover it, a quart of red wine, three anchovies, an onion, two or three blades of mace, some whole pepper and a bunch of sweet herbs; stew it over a slow fire five or six hours, turn it often in the stewing, and keep it close covered; when it is stewed enough, take from it the gravy, thicken part of
it

it with a lump of butter and flour, and put it upon the dish with the beef. Garnish the dish with horse-radish and beet root. There must be no salt upon the beef, only salt the gravy. Send up any kind of greens or roots in a separate dish, as you chuse.

To stew Beef.

Cut raw beef in the manner as you do veal for Scotch collops; lay it in the dish with some water, put to it a shalot, a glass of white wine, some marjoram powdered, some pepper and salt, and a slice or two of fat bacon; then put it over the fire a short time, till your dish is full of gravy, you may put in some catchup, serve it hot, garnish with lemon sliced.

To stew Veal.

Procure some lean veal, either raw, boiled or roasted, and having cut it into thin slices, put them in as much water as will just cover them, then put some pepper and salt, some mace and nutmeg, a shalot, sweet marjoram, and some lemon peel; and when they are stewed near enough, put some mushroom gravy into the liquor, some lemon juice, a glass of white wine, and stew it a little longer, then strain off the liquor, and you may put some pickled mushrooms in the sauce, and thicken your sauce with cream, or butter rolled in flour. Garnish with sliced lemon or orange, and fried oysters.

To stew a Rump, Leg, or Neck of Mutton.

First break the bones, and put them in a pot with some whole pepper, mace and salt, one anchovy,

chovy, one nutmeg, and one turnip, two onions, a bunch of sweet herbs, a pint of ale, a little red wine if you chuse, a quart or two of water and a hard crust of bread; stop it up and let it stew five hours, and serve it with toasts and gravy. Put half this to the mutton, and stew it two hours. You may bake an Ox-cheek in the same manner.

To stew Mutton Chops.

Put them into a shallow tin pan, with a very small quantity of water, and some pepper and salt: cover your pan very close, and place it over a slow fire. When the chops are done (which will be in a very short time) dish them up with their own liquor, and garnish with pickles.

To stew Chickens.

Take two chickens, cut them into quarters, wash them clean, and put them into a sauce-pan; put to them a quarter of a pint of water, half a pint of wine, some mace, pepper, a bundle of sweet herbs, an onion, and a few raspings; cover them close, let them stew half an hour, then take a piece of butter about as big as an egg rolled in flour, put in, and cover it close for five or six minutes, shake the sauce pan about, then take out the sweet herbs and onion. You may take the yolks of two eggs, beat and mixed with them; if you do not like it leave them out. Garnish with lemon.

To stew Ducks whole.

Take ducks when they are drawn and washed clean, put them into a stew-pan with strong broth, red wine, mace, whole pepper, an onion, an anchovy, and lemon peel; when well stewed put in a piece of butter, and some grated bread to thicken it; lay round them crisp bacon and force meat balls. Garnish with shalot.

To stew Pigeons.

Take your pigeons, season and stuff them, flat the breast bone, and truss them up as you would do for baking, dredge them over with some flour, and fry them in butter, turning them round till all sides be brown, then put them into a stew-pan, with as much brown gravy as will cover them, and let it stew till your pigeons be done, then take part of the gravy, an anchovy shred, some catchup, an onion, or a shalot, and some juice of lemon for sauce, pour it over your pigeons, and lay round them forced meat balls and crisp bacon. Garnish your dish with crisp parsley and lemon.

To stew Giblets.

Take the giblets clean picked and washed, the feet skinned and bill cut off, the head cut in two, the pinions and bones sawn in two, the liver cut in two, the gizzard cut into four, the pipe pulled out of the neck, and the neck cut in two; put them into a pipkin with a gill of water, some black and white pepper, a blade of mace, a sprig of thyme, a small onion, a crust of bread, then cover them close, and set them on a slow fire. Let them stew till they are tender, then take out the herbs and onions, and pour them into a dish. Season them with salt.

To stew Rabbits.

Cut your Rabbits into quarters, then lard them with pretty lardoons of bacon, fry them, stew them in a stew-pan with strong broth, white wine, pepper, salt, a faggot of sweet herbs, fried flour and orange.

To stew Trout.

Take a large trout, wash it, and put it in a pan with white wine and gravy, then take for stuffing, two raw eggs, some pepper, salt, nutmeg, lemon peel, grated bread, a little butter or suet, and thyme, mix them all together, and put in the belly of the trout; then let it stew a quarter of an hour, and put a piece of butter into the sauce, serve it hot, and garnish with lemon sliced.

N. B. This will be stuffing for any kind of fish.

To stew Cod.

Lay your cod in thin slices at the bottom of a dish, with half a pint of white wine, a pint of gravy and some oysters with their liquor, some pepper and salt and some nutmeg, let it stew till it is near enough, then thicken it with a piece of butter rolled in flour, let it stew a little longer, serve it hot, and garnish with lemon sliced.

To stew a Carp from PONTAC's.

Take half gravy and half claret, as much as will cover your carp in the pan, with mace, whole pepper, some cloves, two anchovies, some horse radish, a shalot or onion and salt; when the carp is enough, take it out, and boil the liquor as fast as possible, till it be just enough to make sauce; flour a bit of butter, and throw into it the juice of one lemon, then pour it over the carp.

To stew Oysters.

Plump them into their own liquor; then strain them off, wash them in clean water, and take off their beards; then set on some of their own liquor, water and white wine, a blade or two of mace, and some whole pepper; then put in your oysters; let them simmer for 15 minutes or thereabouts, then thicken them with the yolks of two eggs, a piece of butter, some flour, and a little cream, beat up well; thicken it and serve it up with sippets and lemon. Cockles and muscles may be stewed the same way.

To stew a Pike.

Take a large pike, scale and clean it, season it in the belly with some mace and salt, skewer it round, put it into a deep stew-pan, with a pint of small gravy, a pint of red wine, and two or three blades of mace, set it over a stove with a slow fire and cover it up close; when it is stewed enough, take part of the liquor, put to it two anchovies, some lemon peel shred fine, and thicken the sauce with flour and butter; before you lay the pike on the dish turn it with the back upwards, take off the skin and serve it up. Garnish the dish with lemon and pickle.

To stew Tench.

Scale your tench, gut it, and wash the inside with vinegar, then put it into a stew-pan when the water boils, with some salt, a bunch of sweet herbs, some lemon peel and whole pepper; cover it up close and boil it quick till enough, then strain off some of the liquor, and put to it some white wine and walnut liquor, or
mush-

mushroom gravy, an anchovy, some oysters or shrimps; boil these together, toss them up with thick butter rolled in flour, adding some lemon juice. Garnish with lemon, horse radish, and serve it hot with sippits.

To stew Apples.

Take eight or ten large pippins, pared and cut in halves, a pound of fine sugar, and a quart of water; then boil the sugar and water together, skim it, and put your apples in the syrup to boil, covered with froth till they are tender and clear; put some lemon in, and lemon peel cut long and narrow, and a glass of wine; let them give one boil, put it in a china dish and serve it cold.

To stew Pears.

Pare six pears, and either quarter them, or do them whole; they are a pretty dish with one whole, the rest cut in quarters, and the cores taken out. Lay them in a deep earthen pot, with a few cloves, a piece of lemon peel, a gill of red wine, and a quarter of a pound of fine sugar. If the pears are very large, they will take half a pound of sugar, and half a pint of red wine; cover them close with brown paper, and bake them till they are enough. Serve them hot or cold, just as you like them, and they will be very good with water in the place of wine.

To stew Pears in a sauce-pan.

Put them into a sauce-pan, with the ingredients as before; cover them and do them over a slow fire, when they are enough take them off.

To stew Pears purple.

Pare four pears, cut them into quarters, core them, and put them into a stew-pan, with a quarter of a pint of water, a quarter of a pound of sugar, cover them with a pewter plate, then cover the pan with the lid, and do them over a slow fire. Look at them often, for fear of melting the plate; when they are enough, and the liquor looks of a fine purple, take them off, and lay them in your dish with the liquor; when cold serve them up for a side-dish at a second course.

To stew Pippins whole.

Take twelve golden pippins, pare them, and put the parings into a sauce-pan with water enough to cover them, a blade of mace, two or three cloves, a piece of lemon peel, let them simmer till there is just enough to stew the pippins in, then strain it, and put it into the sauce-pan again, with sugar enough to make it like a syrup; then put them into a preserving-pan, or clean stew-pan, or large sauce-pan, and pour the syrup over them. Let there be enough to stew them in; and when they are enough, which you will know by the pippins being soft, take them up, and lay them in a little dish with the syrup: when cold, serve them up; or hot, if you chuse it.

BROILING.

To broil Beef Steaks.

Cut your steaks half an inch thick or thereabouts (off the rump is the best) and beat them, strew

strew them over with some pepper and salt, lay them on your gridiron over a clear fire, turning them often till enough; set your dish over a chafing-dish of coals, with a little brown gravy, chop an onion or shalot small as possible, and put it to the gravy; shake it all together, and put them on a dish. Garnish with shalot and pickles.

To broil Mutton Chops.

Cut your chops off the best end of a neck of mutton, pare them neatly, and flat them with a cleaver; season them with pepper and salt, broil them over a clear fire, turning them often; when done, lay them in a hot dish with some gravy under them, and a spoonful of mushroom catchup, and serve them up hot with pickles in a saucer. You may crumb them with bread, the same as veal cutlets.

To broil Chickens.

Slit them down the back, season them with pepper and salt, lay them on a clear fire at a great distance; let the inside lie next the fire till it is above half done, then turn them, and take great care the fleshy side does not burn; throw some fine raspings of bread over them, and let them be of a fine brown, but not burnt. Let your sauce be good gravy, with mushrooms, and garnish with lemon and the livers broiled, the gizzards cut, flashed, and broiled with pepper and salt.

Or this sauce; take a handful of sorrel, dipped in boiling water, drain it, and have ready half a pint of good gravy, a shalot shred small, and some parsley boiled very green; thicken it with a piece of butter rolled in flour, and add a glaſs of red wine, then lay your ſorrel in heaps round the fowls, and pour the ſauce over them. Garniſh with lemon.

Note, You may make juſt what ſauce you fancy.

To broil Cod-ſounds.

Scald them in hot water, and rub them with ſalt; take off the black dirty ſkin, ſet them on the fire in cold water, and let them ſimmer till they begin to be tender, take them out and flour them, and broil them on a gridiron. For ſauce take a little good gravy, muſtard, pepper and ſalt, a bit of butter rolled in flour, give it a boil, ſeaſon it with pepper and ſalt, lay the ſounds on a diſh, and pour your ſauce over them.

To broil Mackrel.

Clean them, cut off the heads, ſplit them, ſeaſon them with pepper and ſalt, flour them, broil them of a fine light brown, and let your ſauce be plain butter.

To broil Salmon.

Cut it into thick pieces, flour and broil them, lay it in your diſh, and have melted butter in a cup.

To broil Haddocks when in high ſeaſon.

Scale, gut and waſh them clean, don't rip open their bellies, but take the guts out with the gills; dry them in a clean cloth very well: if there be any roe or liver take it out, but put it in again; flour them well, and have a good clear fire. Let your gridiron be hot and clean,

lay

lay them on, turn them quick two or three times for fear of sticking; then let one side be enough, and turn the other side. When that is done, lay them in a dish, and have plain butter in a cup.

They eat finely salted a day or two before you dress them, and hung up to dry, or boiled with egg-sauce.

To broil Whitings.

Wash them with water and salt, then dry them well and flour them; rub your gridiron well with chalk and make it hot; then lay them on, and when they are done, serve them with oyster or shrimp sauce, and garnish with lemon. The chalk will keep the fish from sticking.

To broil Herrings.

Scale them, gut them, cut off their heads, wash them clean, dry them in a cloth, flour them and broil them, but with your knife just notch them across: take the heads and mash them, boil them in small beer or ale, with a little whole pepper and onion. Let it boil a quarter of an hour, then strain it; thicken it with butter and flour, and a good deal of mustard. Lay the fish in the dish, and pour the sauce into a bason, or plain melted butter and mustard.

To broil Eels.

Take a large eel, skin it, and make it clean, open the belly, cut it in four pieces, take the tail end, strip off the flesh, beat it in a mortar, season it with a little beaten mace, a little grated nutmeg, pepper, salt, a little parsley and thyme, a little lemon-peel, an equal quantity of crumbs of bread, roll it in a piece of butter; then mix it again with the yolk of an egg, roll it up again, and fill the three pieces of belly with it, cut the skin of the eel, wrap the pieces in, and sew up the skin, broil them well; have butter and an anchovy for sauce, with the juice of a lemon.

FRYING.

To fry Veal Cutlets.

Cut your veal into slices and lard them with bacon, and season with sweet marjoram, nutmeg, pepper, salt, and a little grated lemon-peel, wash them over with egg, and strew over them this mixture; then fry them in sweet butter, and serve them with lemon sliced and gravy.

Another way of dressing Veal Cutlets.

Cut a neck of veal into steaks, and fry it in butter; boil the scrag to strong broth, and two anchovies, two nutmegs, some lemon-peel, penny-royal, and parsley, shred very small; burn a bit of butter, pour in the liquor and the veal cutlets, with a glass of white wine, and toss them all up together. If it be not thick enough, flour a bit of butter and throw in. Lay it in the dish, squeeze an orange, and strew as much salt as will give them a relish.

To fry Mutton Steaks.

Cut off the rump end of the loin, then cut the rest into steaks and flat them with a cleaver, or a rolling-pin, season them with a little salt and pepper, and fry them in butter over a good fire, as you fry them put them into an earthen pot

pot 'till you have fried them all; then pour the fat out of the pan, put in a little gravy, and the gravy that comes from the steaks, with a spoonful of red wine, an anchovy, and an onion or a shalot shred; shake up the steaks in the gravy, and thicken it up with horse-radish and shalot.

To dress Mutton Cutlets.

First take a handful of grated bread, a little thyme, parsley, and lemon-peel shred small, with some salt, pepper and nutmeg; then cut a loin of mutton into steaks, and let them be well beaten; and the yolks of two eggs, rub all over the steaks. Strew on grated bread with these ingredients mixed together and fry them. Make your sauce of gravy, with a spoonful or two of red wine, and an anchovy.

To fry Beef Steaks with Oysters.

Pepper some tender beef steaks to your mind, but do not salt them, for that will make them hard; turn them often till they are enough, which you will know by their fealing firm, then salt them to your mind.—For sauce take oysters with their liquor, and wash them in salt and water; let the oyster liquor stand to settle, and then pour off the clear; stew them gently in it, with a little nutmeg or mace, some whole pepper, a clove or two, and take care you do not stew them too much, for that will make them hard; when they are almost enough, add a little white wine, and a piece of butter rolled in flour to thicken it. Some chuse to put an anchovy or mushroom catchup into this sauce, which makes it rich.

Another

Another way to fry Beef Steaks.

Take rump steaks, beat them very well with a roller, fry them in half a pint of ale that is not bitter, and whilst they are frying cut a large onion small, a very little thyme, some parsley shred small, some grated nutmeg, and a little pepper and salt; roll all together in a piece of butter, and then put in a little flour, put this into the stew-pan, and shake all together. When the steaks are tender, and the sauce of a fine thickness, dish it up.

Another way to fry Beef Steaks.

Cut the lean by itself, and beat them well with the back of a knife, fry them in just as much butter as will moisten the pan, pour out the gravy as it runs out of the meat, turn them often, do them over a gentle fire, then fry the fat by itself and lay upon the meat, and put to the gravy a glass of red wine, half an anchovy, a little nutmeg, a little beaten pepper, and a shalot cut small; give it two or three little boils, season it with salt to your palate, pour it over the steaks, and send them to table.

To fry a Loin of Lamb.

Cut the loin into thin steaks, put a very little pepper and salt, a little nutmeg on them, and fry them in fresh butter; when enough, take out the steaks, lay them in a dish before the fire to keep hot, then pour out the butter, shake a little flour over the bottom of the pan, pour in a quarter of a pint of boiling water, and put in a piece of butter; shake all together, give it a boil,

boil, pour it our the steaks, and send it to table. You may do mutton the same way, and add two spoonfuls of walnut pickle.

To fry Calves Feet in Butter.

Take four calves feet and blanch them, boil them as you would do for eating, take out the large bones and cut them in two, beat a spoonful of wheat flour and four eggs together, put to it some nutmeg, pepper and salt, dip in your calves feet, and fry them in butter a light brown, lay them upon a dish with some melted butter, garnish with slices of lemon, and serve them up.

To fry Sausages.

Take half a pound of sausages, and six apples, slice four about as thick as a crown, cut the other two in quarters, fry them with the sausages of a fine light brown, lay the sausages in the middle of the dish, and the apples round. Garnish with the quartered apples.

To fry Carp.

First scale and gut them, wash them clean, lay them in a cloth to dry, then flour them, and fry them of a light brown. Fry some toast cut three-corner-ways, and the roes; when your fish is done, lay them on a coarse cloth to drain. Let your sauce be butter and anchovy, with the juice of lemon. Lay your carp in the dish, the roes on each side, and garnish with fry'd toast and lemon.

To fry Herrings.

Clean them as above, fry them in butter, have ready a good many onions peeled and cut thin.

thin. Fry them of a light brown with the herrings; lay the herrings in your dish, and the onions round, and butter and muſtard in a cup. You muſt do them with a quick fire.

To fry Lampreys.

Bleed them and fave the blood, then waſh them in hot water to take of the ſlime, and cut them to pieces. Fry them in a little freſh butter not quite enough, pour out the fat, put in a little white wine, give the pan a ſhake round, ſeaſon it with whole pepper, nutmeg, ſalt, ſweet herbs, and a bay-leaf, put in a few capers, a good piece of butter rolled in flour, and the blood; give the pan a ſhake round often, and cover them cloſe. When you think they are enough take them out, ſtrain the ſauce, and give them a quick boil, ſqueeze in a little lemon and pour it over the fiſh. Garniſh with lemon, and dreſs them juſt what way you fancy.

To fry Eels.

Make them very clean, cut them into pieces, ſeaſon them with pepper and ſalt, flour and fry them in butter. Let your ſauce be plain butter melted, with the juice of lemon. Be ſure they be well drained from the fat before you lay them in the diſh.

To fry Oyſters.

Make a batter of milk, flour and eggs, then take ſome oyſters, waſh and dry them, dip them in the batter; then roll them in ſome crumbs of bread and mace beat fine, and fry them in hot lard or butter.

To

To fry Pancakes.

Take a pint of milk or cream, eight eggs, a nutmeg grated, and some salt; then melt one pound of butter, and a little sack, before you stir it; it must be as thick with flour as ordinary butter, and fried with lard, turn it on the back-side of a plate. Garnish with orange, and strew sugar over them.

To make Apple Fritters.

Take the whites of three eggs and the yolks of six beat well together, and put to them a pint of milk or cream; then put to it four or five spoonfuls of flour, a glass of brandy, half a nutmeg grated, and some ginger and salt, your batter must be pretty thick, then slice your apples in rounds, and dipping each round in batter, fry them in good lard, over a quick fire.

To make white Scotch Collops.

Cut about four pounds of a fillet of veal into thin pieces, then take a clean stew pan, butter it over, and shake some flour over it; then lay your meat in piece by piece, till all your pan is covered; then take two or three blades of mace, and a little nutmeg, set your stew pan over the fire, toss it up together till all your meat be white; then take half a pint of strong veal broth, which must be ready made, a quarter of a pint of cream, and the yolks of two eggs, mix all these together, put to it the meat, keep it tossing all the time till they just boil up, when enough squeeze in some lemon; add oysters and mushrooms to make it rich.

To make an Apple Tansey.

Cut three or four pippins into thin slices, and fry them in good butter, then beat four eggs with six spoonfuls of cream, some rose-water, sugar and nutmeg, stir them together, and pour it over the apples; let it fry a little, and turn it with a pie-plate. Garnish with lemon, and sugar strewed over it.

To make a Gooseberry Tansey.

Fry a quart of gooseberries till tender in fresh butter, and mash them; then beat seven or eight eggs, four or five whites, a pound of sugar; three spoonfuls of sack, as much cream, a penny loaf grated, and three spoonfuls of flour; mix all these together, put the gooseberries out of the pan to them, stir all well together, and put them into a sauce-pan to thicken; then put fresh butter into a frying-pan, fry them brown, and strew sugar over the top.

To make a Water Tansey.

Take a dozen eggs and eight or nine of the whites, beat them very well, and grate a penny loaf, and put in a quarter of a pound of melted butter, and a pint of the juice of spinage, then sweeten it to your taste.

To make Apple Froise.

Cut your apples into thin slices, then fry them of a light brown; take them up and lay them to drain, and keep them from breaking, then make the following batter: take five eggs, but three whites, beat them up with flour and cream, and a little sack; make it the thickness of a pancake

cake batter, pour in a little melted butter, nutmeg, and a little sugar. Melt your butter and pour batter, and lay a slice of apple here and there, pour more batter on them; fry them a light brown, then take them up, and strew fine sugar over them.

BAKING.
For baking Beef the French way.

First bone it, and take away the skin and sinews, then lard it with fat bacon, season your beef with cloves, salt and pepper; then tie it up tight with a pack-thread, and put it in an earthen pan, some whole pepper, an onion stuck with ten cloves, and put at the top a bunch of sweet herbs, two or three bay-leaves, a quarter of a pound of butter, and half a pint of red, or white wine; cover it close, bake it four or five hours, then serve it hot with its own liquor, or cold in slices, to be eat with mustard and vinegar.

To bake a Leg of Beef.

Take a leg of beef, cut and hack it, put it into a large earthen pan; put to it a bundle of sweet herbs, two onions stuck with a few cloves, a blade or two of mace, a piece of carrot, a spoonful of whole pepper black and white, and a quart of stale beer. Cover it with water, tie the pot down close with brown paper rubbed with butter, send it to the oven, and let it be well baked. When it comes home, strain it through a coarse sieve. Pick out all the sinews and fat, put them into a sauce-pan with a few spoonfuls of the gravy, a little red wine, a little piece of
butter

butter rolled in flour, and some mustard; shake your sauce-pan often, and when the sauce is hot and thick, dish it up, and send it to table. It is a pretty dish.

For baking a Calf's Head.

First wash it clean, then halve it, and beat the yolks of three eggs, and rub it over with a feather on the backside, then take some grated bread, pepper, salt, and nutmeg, lemon peel grated, and some sage cut small; then strew it over the outside of the head, lay it in an earthen dish, and cover the head with bits of butter, put a little water in the dish, and bake it in a quick oven; when you serve it, pour over it some strong gravy, with the brains first boiled and mixed in it. Garnish with lemon.

To bake an Ox's Head.

Do just in the same manner as the leg of beef is directed to be done, in making the gravy as before, and it does full as well for the same uses. If it is too strong for any thing you want it for, it is only putting some hot water to it. Cold water will spoil it.

To bake a Pig.

If you should be in a place where you cannot roast a pig, lay it in a dish, flour it all over well, and rub it over with butter*; butter the dish you lay it in, and put it into an oven. When it is enough draw it out of the oven's mouth, and rub it over with a buttery cloth; then put it into the oven again 'till it is dry, take it out, and

---

* Florence oil may be used with the greatest propriety instead of butter, some think the flavour more exquisite.

and lay it in a diſh; cut it up, take a little veal gravy, and take off the fat in the diſh it was baked in, and there will be ſome good gravy at the bottom, put that to it, with a piece of butter rolled in flour; boil it up, and put it into the diſh with the brains and ſage in the belly. Some love a pig brought whole to table, then you are only to put what ſauce you like into the diſh.

To bake a Turbot.

Take a diſh the ſize of your turbot, rub butter all over it thick, throw a little beaten pepper and ſalt, half a large nutmeg, and ſome parſley minced fine over it, pour in a pint of white wine, cut off the head and tail, lay the turbot in the diſh, pour another pint of white wine all over, grate the other half of the nutmeg over it, and a little pepper, ſome ſalt and a little chopped parſley. Lay a piece of butter here and there all over, and throw a little flour over all, and then a good many crumbs of bread. Bake it, and be ſure that it is of a fine brown; then lay it in your diſh, ſtir the ſauce in your diſh all together, pour it into a ſauce-pan, ſhake in a little flour, let it boil, then ſtir in a piece of butter and two ſpoonfuls of catchup, let it boil and pour it into baſons. Garniſh your diſh with lemon; and you may add what you fancy to the ſauce, as ſhrimps, anchovies, muſhrooms, &c. If a ſmall turbot, half the wine will do. It eats finely thus: lay it in a diſh, ſkim off all the fat, and pour the reſt over it. Let it ſtand till cold, and it is good with vinegar, and a fine diſh to ſet out a cold table.

To bake Herrings.

Put fifty herrings into a pan, cover them with two parts water, and one part vinegar, with a good deal of all-spice, some cloves, a bunch of sweet herbs, a few bay-leaves, and two large onions, tie them down close, and bake them; when they come out of the oven, heat a pint of red wine hot, and put to them; then tie them down again, and let them stand four or five days before you open them, and they will be very fine and firm.

To bake any sort of Fish.

Butter the pan, lay in the fish, throw a little salt and flour over it, put a very little water in the dish, an onion and a bundle of sweet herbs; stick some little bits of butter on the fish, and let it be baked of a fine light brown; when enough, lay it on a dish before the fire, and skim off all the fat in the pan, strain the liquor, and mix it up either with the fish-sauce or strong soup, or catchup.

To bake Mutton Chops.

Take a loin or neck of mutton, cut it in thin steaks, put some pepper and salt over it, butter your dish and lay in your steaks; then take a quart of milk, six eggs beat up fine, and four spoonfuls of flour; beat your flour and eggs in a little milk first, and then put the rest to it; put in a little beaten ginger, and a little salt. Pour this over the steaks, and send it to the oven; an hour and an half will bake it.

FRICASSEES.

To fricaſſee Lamb.

Cut a hind quarter of lamb into thin ſlices, ſeaſon them with ſavoury ſpice, ſweet herbs, and a ſhalot; then fry them, toſs them up in ſtrong broth, white wine, oyſters, two palates, a little brown batter, force-meat balls, and an egg or two to thicken it, or a bit of butter rolled in flour. Garniſh with lemon.

To fricaſſee Lamb-ſtones and Sweetbreads.

Have ready ſome lamb-ſtones blanched, parboiled and ſliced, and flour two or three ſweetbreads; if very thick, cut them in two, the yolks of ſix hard eggs whole; a few piſtacho-nut kernels, and a few large oyſters: fry theſe all of a fine brown, then pour out all the butter, and add a pint of drawn gravy, the lamb-ſtones, ſome aſparagus tops about an inch long, ſome grated nutmeg, a little pepper and ſalt, two ſhalots ſhred ſmall, and a glaſs of white wine. Stew all theſe together for ten minutes, then add the yolks of ſix eggs beat very fine, with a little white wine, and a little beaten mace; ſtir all together till it is of a fine thickneſs, and then diſh it up. Garniſh with lemon.

To fricaſſee cold Roaſt Beef.

Firſt cut your beef into thin ſlices, then ſhred a handful of parſley very ſmall, cut an onion into pieces and put them together in a ſtew-pan, with a piece of butter, and a good quantity of ſtrong broth; ſeaſon with pepper and ſalt; let it ſtew

stew gently a quarter of an hour, then beat the yolk of four eggs in some red wine, and a spoonful of vinegar, put it to your meat, and stir it till it grows thick. Rub your dish with a shalot before you serve it up.

To fricassee Calf's Feet white.

Boil the feet as you would do for eating, then take out the bones, and cut them in two, put them into a stew-pan, with a little white gravy, and a spoonful of white wine; take the yolks of three eggs, three spoonfuls of cream, grate a little nutmeg and salt, with a lump of butter; shake all well together, and garnish your dish with slices of lemon and currants.

To make a brown fricassee of Rabbits or Chickens.

You must take your rabbits or chickens and skin them, then cut them into small pieces, and rub them over with yolks of eggs; have ready some grated bread, a little beaten mace, and a little grated nutmeg, and then roll them in it; put a little butter into a stew-pan, and when it is melted put in your meat; fry it of a fine brown, and take care they do not stick to the bottom of the pan, then pour the butter from them, and pour in half a pint of gravy, a glass of red wine, a few mushrooms, or two spoonfuls of the pickle, a little salt (if wanted) and a piece of butter rolled in flour; when it is of a fine thickness dish it up, and send it to table.

To make a white fricassee of Rabbits, Chickens, Veal, &c.

Skin them and cut them into small pieces, lay them

them into warm water to draw out the blood, and then lay them in a cloth to dry; put them into a stew-pan with milk and water, stew them till they are tender, then take a clean pan, put in half a pint of cream, and a quarter of a pound of butter, stir it together till it is melted, but be sure to keep it stirring all the time or it will be greasy; then with a fork take the chickens or rabbits out of the stew-pan, and put them into the sauce-pan to the butter and cream; have ready a little mace dried and beat fine, a little nutmeg, a few mushrooms, shake all together for a minute or two, and dish it up. This is a pretty sauce for a breast of veal roasted. You may fricassee veal, lamb, mutton, &c. the same way.

To fricassee Pigeons.

Take eight pigeons, new killed, cut them into small pieces, and put them into a stew-pan with a pint of claret and a pint of water; season your pigeons with salt and pepper, a blade or two of mace, an onion, a bundle of sweet herbs, a good piece of butter rolled in a very little flour; cover it close, and let them stew till there is just enough for sauce, then take out the onion and sweet herbs; beat up the yolks of three eggs, grate half a nutmeg in, and with your spoon push the meat all to one side of the pan, and the gravy to the other side, and stir in the eggs; keep them stirring for fear of turning to curds, and when the sauce is fine and thick, shake all together, put in half a spoonful of vinegar, and give them another shake; then put the meat into the dish, pour the sauce over it,

and

and have ready some slices of bacon toasted, and fried oysters. Throw the oysters all over, lay the bacon round, and garnish with lemon.

To fricassee Ducks.

Quarter them and beat them with the back of your cleaver, dry them well, fry them in sweet butter, and when they are almost fried, put in a handful of onions shred small, and a little thyme; then put in a little red wine, some thin slices of bacon, with spinage and parsley boiled green and shred small; break the yolks of three eggs, with a little pepper in a dish, and some grated nutmeg, tofs them up with a ladle-full of drawn butter, pour this over ducks, lay your bacon upon them, and serve it hot.

To fricassee a Goose.

Roast your goose, and before it is quite done, cut and notch it with a knife long-ways, then flash it across, and strew pepper and salt over it, then lay it in your pan, with the skinny side downwards, till it has taken a gentle heat, then broil it on a gridiron over a gentle fire; when it is enough baste the upper side with butter, a little sugar, vinegar and mustard; pour this into a dish, with sausages and lemons, and serve it up.

To fricassee Cod-sounds.

Clean them well, then cut them into little pieces, boil them tender in milk and water, then throw them into a cullender to drain, pour them into a clean sauce-pan, season them with a little beaten mace and grated nutmeg, and a very

little

little falt; pour to them juft cream enough for fauce, and a good piece of butter rolled in flour; keep fhaking your fauce-pan round all the time, till it is thick enough, then difh it up. Garnifh with lemon.

To fricaffee Artichoke-bottoms.

Take them either dried or pickled; if dried, you muft lay them in warm water for three or four hours, fhifting the water two or three times; then have ready a little cream, and a piece of frefh butter, ftirring together one way over the fire till it is melted, then put in the artichokes, and when they are hot difh them up.

To make Force-meat Balls.

Take half a pound of fuet, as much veal cut fine, and beat it in a marble mortar; have a few fweet herbs fhred fine, a little mace dried and beat fine, a fmall nutmeg grated, fome pepper and falt, add the yolks of two eggs; mix all thefe well together, roll them in flour, and fry them brown. If they are for white fauce, put them into a fauce-pan, and let them boil a few minutes; but never fry them for white fauce.

To fricaffee a Calf's Head.

Your head muft be well cleaned and boiled tender; then cut it in fquare pieces as big as a walnut; then tofs it up with mufhrooms, fweetbreads and artichoke bottoms, cream and the yolks of eggs; feafon it with mace and nutmeg, and fqueeze in a lemon, fo ferve away hot.

To

To fricassee double Tripe.

Clean your tripe well, and boil it tender, take the double part, and cut it in pieces two inches long; put a lump of butter in a stew-pan, with two shalots cut very small, give it a toss on the fire, put in your tripe, dust it with flour, add to it half a pint of broth, and a glass of white wine, season them with pepper, salt, and a bunch of sweet herbs; let them stew softly, and let them have a good taste; thicken up your sauce with the yolks of two eggs well beaten, add a little parsley cut small, and a little nutmeg; mix your eggs with a little broth and juice of lemon, and put it to your tripe; let it just simmer, dish it up, and serve it up for a small entry.

To fricassee Sturgeon brown.

Cut your sturgeon in thin slices, and season it with pepper, salt, and nutmeg, strew over a little flour, and fry it brownish; then take a bit of butter, pass it brown with flour; put in some good gravy, one anchovy, and the juice of an orange; so serve away.

Directions for making Pyes, Tarts, &c.

Observations on Pyes.

ALL raised pyes must be made the night before baking, otherwise they are in danger of falling in the oven; little gravy is required, or it will either force its way out, or crack the sides of the pye: But you must, after the pye comes from the oven, warm your gravy and pour it in. Pyes of all kinds require a quick oven. But puff pyes require not so hot an oven, or they burn; therefore a medium is to be observed, as in a slow oven they will become sad and not rise.

A good crust for great Pyes.

To a peck of flour add the yolks of three eggs; then boil some water, and put in half a pound of fried suet, and a pound and half of butter. Skim off the butter and suet, and as much of the liquor as will make it a light good crust: work it up well, and roll it out.

A standing crust for great Pyes.

Take a peck of flour, and six pounds of butter, boiled in a gallon of water; skim it off into the flour, and as little of the liquor as you can; work it well up into a paste, then pull it into pieces till it is cold, then make it up in what form you will have it. This is fit for the walls of a goose pye.

Cold paste for all sorts of dished Pyes.

Take two pounds of flour, make a hole in the middle, put in one pound of butter, and a little water, make it into a paste, but do not work it much, then roll it out, dust on some flour, wrap it up again, and roll it out for use.

Another way.

Rub six ounces of butter into two pounds of flour, add to it one egg, and as much water as will make it into a paste; roll it out, lay on it fifteen ounces of butter, with a little flour, and roll it out twice for use.

A dripping Crust.

Take a pound and half of beef-dripping, boil it in water, strain it, then let it stand to be cold, and take off the hard fat, scrape it, boil it so four or five times; then work it well up into three pounds of flour, as fine as you can, and make it up into paste with cold water. It makes a very fine crust.

To make a Beef Steak Pye.

Take fine rump steaks, beat them, then season them

them with pepper and salt, and shalot to your liking shred fine, make a good crust, lay in your steaks, with a quarter of a pound of butter at top, fill your dish, pour in as much water as will half fill the dish, put on the crust, and bake it well.

To make a Mutton Pye.

Pepper and salt your mutton steaks, fill the pye, then lay on butter, pour in some thin gravy and close it. When it is baked, skim the fat off the pye, toss up a handful of chopped capers, oysters, and cucumbers in gravy, an anchovy, and drawn butter, and pour them in.

To make a savoury Lamb Pye.

First season the lamb with pepper, salt, cloves, mace, and nutmeg, then put it into your crust, with a few sweet-breads and lamb-stones, seasoned as your lamb, also some oysters, add savoury force-meat balls, hard yolks of eggs, and pour in a little thin gravy; then put butter all over the pye, and lid it, and set it in a quick oven an hour and a half; then make a lare with oyster liquor, as much gravy, some claret with one anchovy in it, and a grated nutmeg. Let these have a boil, thicken it with the yolks of two or three eggs, and when the pye is drawn put it in.

To make a pretty sweet Lamb or Veal Pye.

Make a good crust, butter the dish, and lay in your bottom and side-crust, then cut your meat in small pieces, season with a very little salt, some mace and nutmeg beat fine, and strewed over; then lay a lare of meat, and strew some

some currants clean washed and picked, and a few raisins stoned, all over the meat; lay another lare of meat, put a little butter at the top, and a little water just enough to bake it and no more. Have ready against it comes out of the oven, a white wine caudle made very sweet, and send it to table hot.

To make a very fine sweet Lamb or Veal Pye.

Season your lamb with salt, pepper, cloves, mace, and nutmeg, all beat fine, to your palate, cut your lamb or veal into little pieces, make a good puff-paste crust, lay it in your dish, then lay in your meat, strew on it some stoned raisins and currants clean washed, and some sugar; then lay on it some force-meat balls made sweet, and in the summer some artichoke-bottoms boiled, and scalded grapes in the winter. Boil Spanish potatoes cut in pieces, candied citron, candied orange, and lemon-peel, and three or four blades of mace, put butter on the top, close up your pye, and bake it. Have ready against it comes out of the oven, a caudle made thus: Take a pint of white wine, and mix in the yolks of three eggs, stir it well together over the fire, one way all the time till it is thick; then take it off, stir in sugar enough to sweeten it, and squeeze in the juice of a lemon; pour it hot into your pye, and close it up again. Send it hot to table.

A raised sweet Pye.

Cut the best end of a neck of veal, season it as above, have ready a coffin made of hot paste, lay in your steaks with a quarter of a pound of currants washed clean, a quarter of a pound of jar raisins stoned, a good slice of butter, and half a pint of veal gravy; cover it up, and ornament it; bind it round with paper, to keep it from falling, bake it two hours, and serve it up either hot or cold.

To make a savoury Lamb or Veal Pye.

Make a good puff-paste crust, cut your meat into pieces, season it to your palate with pepper, salt, mace, cloves, and nutmeg finely beat; lay it into your crust with a few lamb-stones and sweetbreads seasoned as your meat, also some oysters and forced meat-balls, hard yolks of eggs, and the tops of asparagus two inches long, first boiled green; put butter all over the pye, put on the lid and set it in a quick oven an hour and a half, and then have ready the liquor, made thus: Take a pint of gravy, the oyster liquor, a gill of wine, and a little grated nutmeg; mix all together with the yolks of two or three eggs beat, and keep it stirring one way all the time. When it boils, pour it into your pye; put on the lid again. Send it hot to table. You must make liquor according to your pye.

To make a Venison Pasty*.

Lay down half a peck of flour, put to it four pounds of butter, beat eight eggs, and make the paste

---

* When your venison is not fat enough, take the fat of a loin of mutton, steeped in a little rape vinegar and red wine twenty-four hours, then lay it on the top of the venison, and close your pasty. It is a wrong notion of some people to think venison cannot be baked enough, and will first bake it in a false crust, and then bake it in the pasty; by this time the fine flavour of the venison is gone. No, if you want it to be very tender, wash it in warm milk and
water,

paste with warm water, bone the venison, break the bones, season them with salt and pepper, and boil them, with this fill up the pasty when it comes out of the oven; take a pound of beef suet, cut it into long slices, and strew pepper and salt upon it; lay the venison in, seasoned pretty high with salt and black pepper bruised; set pudding crust round the inside of the pasty, and put in about three quarters of a pint of water; lay on a lare of fresh butter, and cover it. When it comes out of the oven, pour in the liquor made of the bones boiled, and shake all together.

To make a Venison Pye.

When you have raised a high pye, shred a pound of beef suet, and lay it in the bottom, cut the venison in pieces, and season it with salt and pepper, lay it on the suet. Lay butter on the venison, close up the pye, and let it stand in the oven for six hours.

water, dry it in clean cloths till it is very dry, then rub it all over with vinegar, and hang it in the air. Keep it as long as you think proper, it will keep thus a fortnight good; but be sure there be no moistness about it; if there is, you must dry it well and throw ginger over it, and it will keep a long time. When you use it, just dip it in lukewarm water, and dry it. Bake it in a quick oven; if it is a large pasty, it will take three hours; then your venison will be tender, and have all the fine flavour. The shoulder makes a pretty pasty boned, and made as above with the mutton fat.

A loin of mutton makes a fine pasty: take a large fat loin of mutton, let it hang four or five days, then bone it, leaving the meat as whole as you can; lay the meat twenty-four hours in half a pint of red wine and half a pint of rape vinegar; then take it out of the pickle, and order it as you do a pasty, and boil the bones in the same manner, to fill the pasty, when it comes out of the oven.

To make a Cheshire Pork Pye.

Take a loin of pork, skin it, cut it into steaks, season it with salt, nutmeg, and pepper; make a good crust, lay a lare of pork, then a large lare of pippins pared and cored, a little sugar, enough to sweeten the pye, then another lare of pork; put in half a pint of white wine, lay some butter on the top, and close your pye. If your pye be large, it will take a pint of white wine.

To make a Calf's Foot Pye.

First set four calves feet on in a sauce-pan in three quarts of water, with three or four blades of mace; let them boil softly till there is about a pint and a half, then take out your feet, strain the liquor, and make a good crust; cover your dish, strew half a pound of currants clean washed and picked over, and half a pound of raisins stoned; lay on the rest of the meat, skim the liquor, sweeten it to the palate, and put in half a pint of white wine; pour it into the dish, put on your lid, and bake it an hour and a half.

To make an Olive Pye.

Make your crust ready, then take the thin collops of the best end of a leg of veal, as many as you think will fill your pye; hack them with the back of a knife, and season them with salt, pepper, cloves, and mace: wash over your collops with a bunch of feathers dipped in eggs, and have in readiness a good handful of sweet-herbs shred small. The herbs must be thyme, parsley, and spinage, the yolks of eight hard eggs minced, and a few oysters parboiled and chopped, some beef suet shred very fine; mix these

these together, and strew them over your collops, then strinkle a little orange-flour water over them, roll the collops up very close, and lay them in your pye, strewing the seasoning over what is left; put butter on the top, and close your pye. When it comes out of the oven, have ready some hot gravy, and pour it into the pye, with an anchovy dissolved in it. You may leave out the orange-flour water if you chuse.

To make a Calf's Head Pye.

Cleanse and wash the head well, boil it for three quarters of an hour, cut the flesh into pieces, blanch the tongue and slice it; parboil a quart of oysters and beard them; take the yolks of ten or twelve eggs, intermix some thin slices of bacon with the meat; put an onion cut small in the bottom of the pye, seasoning it with salt, pepper, nutmeg and mace; lay also butter on the bottom, put in your meat, close up the pye, and put in a little water. When it is baked take off the lid; take off the fat, and put in a lare of thick butter, mutton gravy, a lemon pared and sliced, with two or three anchovies dissolved; let them stew a little while, cut the lid in handsome pieces, lay it round the pye and serve it up.

Another way.

Take a calf's head with the skin on, scald it, take the hair clean off it, split and wash it, and boil it 'till tender; cut the meat clean off the bone as big as a walnut, put into a stew-pan with one quart of gravy, half an anchovy, two glasses of Madeira wine, a little Cayen, beaten mace,

mace, and cloves, a dozen force-meat balls, and a little soy or catchup; let it simmer for half an hour; put to it a piece of butter and flour, squeeze in a little lemon juice; have ready a deep dish sheeted with light paste, put in as many of the bones of the calf's head as will fill it, and a little broth or water, to save your dish; lid it with light paste, and mark it neatly round the edges; bake it in a sharp oven, till the paste is enough; take it out, and cut the lid round within the rim of your dish, take out the bones, and let your hash be quite hot and well seasoned with pepper and salt; put your hash into the dish, lay the lid on it, and serve it up hot. This is a genteel dish for a second course.

To make a Devonshire squab Pye.

Make a good crust, cover the dish all over, put at the bottom a lare of sliced pippins, strew over them some sugar, then a lare of mutton steaks cut from the loin, well seasoned with pepper and salt, then another lare of pippins; peel some onions and slice them thin, lay a lare all over the apples, then a lare of mutton, then pippins and onions, pour in a pint of water; close your pye and bake it.

To make a Shropshire Pye.

Make good puff-paste crust; cut two rabbits into pieces, and two pounds of fat pork into little pieces; season both to your liking; cover your dish with crust, and lay in your rabbits; mix the pork with them; take the livers of the rabbits, parboil them, and beat them in a mortar, with as much fat bacon, a little sweet herbs, and some oysters if you have them. Season with pepper, salt and
nutmeg,

nutmeg, mix it up with the yolk of an egg, and make it into balls; lay them here and there in your pye, fome artichoke bottoms cut in dice, and cocks-combs, if you have them; grate a fmall nutmeg over the meat, then pour in half a pint of red wine, and half a pint of water; clofe your pye, and bake it an hour and a half in a quick oven, but not too fierce an oven.

To make a Yorkshire Christmas Pye.

First make a good ftanding cruft, let the wall and bottom be very thick; bone a turkey, a goofe, a fowl, a partridge, and a pigeon; feafon them all very well, take half an ounce of mace, half an ounce of nutmegs, a quarter of an ounce of cloves, and half an ounce of black pepper, all beat fine together, two large fpoonfuls of falt, and then mix them together; open the fowls down the back, and bone them; firft the pigeon, then the partridge, cover them; then the fowl, then the goofe, and then the turkey, which muft be large; feafon them well, and lay them in the cruft, fo as it will look only like a whole turkey; then have a hare ready cafed, and wiped with a clean cloth, cut it to pieces, that is, joint it; feafon it, and lay it as clofe as you can on one fide; on the other fide woodcocks, moor game, and what fort of wild fowl you can get; feafon them well, and lay them clofe; put at leaft four pounds of butter in the pye, then lay on your lid, which muft be a very thick one, and let it be well baked. It muft have a very hot oven, and will take at leaft four hours.

The cruft will take a bufhel of flour.

To make a Rabbit Pye.

Parboil a couple of rabbits, bone, lard, and season them with pepper, salt, nutmeg, cloves, mace, and winter-savoury; put them in the pye, with a good many force-meat balls, laying a pound of butter on the top, close it up, bake it, and when it is cold, fill it up with clarified butter; and if you chuse, a few bars of bacon at the top.

To make a Hare Pye.

Dress a large Hare, mince one part of it small with bacon, thyme, savoury and marjoram; season it with salt, pepper, cloves and nutmeg; season the other part as you did the former; work the minced meat with the yolks of eggs, and lay it about the hare, and fill up the pye with sweet butter; bake it, and when it comes out of the oven, pour in half a pint of strong gravy.

To make a Goose Pye.

Make the walls that your crust be just big enough to hold the goose; first have a pickled dried tongue, boiled very tender so as to peel, cut off the root, bone the goose, and a large fowl; take half a quarter of an ounce of mace beat fine, three tea spoonfuls of salt, a tea spoonful of beaten pepper, and mix all together; season both fowl and goose with it, then put the fowl into the goose, and the tongue into the fowl, and lay the goose in the same form as if whole; put half a pound of butter on the top, and lay on the lid. This pye is excellent either hot or cold, and may be kept a great while; a slice cut down cross makes a pretty side-dish for supper.

N. B. Half a peck of flour will make the walls
of

of a goose pye, made according to the receipts for crust.

To make a Giblet Pye.

Take two pair of giblets nicely cleaned, put all but the livers into a sauce-pan, with two quarts of water, twenty corns of whole pepper, three blades of mace, a bundle of sweet herbs, and a large onion; cover them close, and let them stew very softly till they are quite tender, then have a good crust ready, cover your dish, lay a fine rump steak at the bottom, seasoned with pepper and salt; then lay in your giblets with the livers, and strain the liquor they were stewed in; season it with salt, and pour in your pye; put on the lid, and bake it an hour and a half.

To make a Green Goose Pye.

Take two fat green geese, bone them, season them pretty high with pepper, salt, and nutmeg, and cloves, and if you like it, add a couple of whole onions in the seasoning, lay them one on another, and fill the sides, then cover them with butter, and send it to the oven.

To make a Turkey Pye.

Raise a neat coffin of hot paste, bone your turkey, season it with savoury spices, add one pound of ham cut in slices, a little force-meat, a litle gravy, and half a pound of butter; close up the pye, ornament it, and set it in the oven, where two hours will bake it.

Another way.

Raise a coffin for it as above, and cut your turkey

turkey up as for eating; season it with pepper, salt, mace, cloves, and nutmeg, lay it in the coffin with some slices of ham, and a pound of butter; close it up, ornament it neatly, bake it two hours and a half, and serve it up cold.

To make a Chicken Pye.

Boil young chickens in an equal quantity of milk and water, then flea them, and season them with salt, cloves and nutmeg; put puff-paste round, and in the bottom of the dish lay a lare of butter, with artichoke bottoms, veal sweet-breads and cocks-combs, and over them lay the chickens, with some bits of butter rolled up in the seasoning, and some balls of force-meat; lay on a lid of puff-paste; the oven must not be too hot. While it is baking make the following caudle: boil a blade of mace in half a pint of white wine or cyder; take it off the fire and slip in the yolks of two eggs well beaten, with a spoonful of sugar, and a bit of butter rolled up in flour. Pour this caudle into the pye when it comes out of the oven.

Another way.

Clean and pick three chickens, cut them in pieces, season them with pepper, salt, and mace; sheet your dish with light paste, lay in the chickens with a little force-meat, a little butter and gravy, close it up, and bake it an hour and a half.

Another way.

Take two chickens, let them be drawn and made clean, cut them in pieces, season them with pepper, salt, and mace; raise a neat coffin
for

for it, lay in the chickens with a pound of ham cut in flices, and fome butter, clofe it up, and bake it two hours. You may ferve it up either hot or cold. If you ferve it up hot, put in half a pint of gravy: if cold, pour in half a pound of clarified butter.

Chicken Pye in fummer.

Cut three chickens as for a fricaffee, well cleaned and picked; feafon with falt, pepper, and mace to your tafte; make a ftanding cafe of hot pafte; and put in the chickens with a little good broth, and let it bake for two hours in the oven. Make ready a gill of green peas boiled tender, a gill of cream boiled ten minutes, and throw in the peas with a piece of butter and flour, a little falt and nutmeg; let them fimmer about five minutes, raife up the lid of your pye, pour it in, with a little juice of lemon, and fend it to table.

A rabbit pye may be made in the fame manner.

To make a Duck Pye.

Take two ducks, fcald them and make them very clean, cut off the feet, pinions, neck and head, with the gizzards, livers and hearts; pick out all the fat of the infide, lay a cruft over the difh, feafon the ducks with pepper and falt infide and out, lay them in your difh, and the giblets at each end feafoned; put in as much water as will almoft fill the pye, lay on the cruft, and bake it, but not too much.

To make a young Rook Pye.

Take young rooks, flea and parpoil them, put

put a crust at the bottom of your dish, with a great deal of butter, and forced-meat balls, then season the rooks with salt, pepper, cloves, mace, nutmeg and some sweet herbs, and put them in your dish; pour in some of the liquor they were parboiled in, and lid it; when baked, cut it open and skim off the fat; warm and pour in the remainder of the liquor, if the pye wants it.

To make a Pigeon Pye.

Make a good crust, cover your dish, let your pigeons be very nicely picked and cleaned, season them with pepper and salt, and put a good piece of butter, with seasoning in their bellies; lay them on the dish, the necks, gizzards, livers, pinions and heart, lay between; with the yolk of a hard egg and beef-steak in the middle; put as much water as will almost fill the dish, lay on the top crust, and bake it well.

Another way.

Pick, draw, and singe six pigeons, season them with pepper and salt, chop the livers with a little fat bacon, thyme and parsley, put a piece into every pigeon, lay them into a dish sheeted with light paste, with half a dozen hard yolks of eggs, six artichoke bottoms boiled tender, and six ounces of butter; sprinkle on a little flour, add some gravy, close up the pye, and bake it one hour and a half.

To make a Lark or Sparrow Pye.

You must have five dozen at least, lay betwixt every one a bit of bacon, and a leaf of sage and a little force-meat at the bottom of your crust; put

put some butter on the top, and lid it. When baked for one hour, which will be sufficient, make a little thickened gravy, put in the juice of a lemon, season with pepper and salt, and serve it hot and quick.

To make minced Pyes.

Parboil the best part of a neat's tongue, peel and cut it in thin slices, and set it to cool. To a pound of beef, tongue, or veal, put two pounds of beef suet, then chop them all together very fine; to each pound of meat put a pound of stoned raisins, and a pound of currants chopped small; then pound your spice, which must be cloves, mace and nutmeg; season it as you like with sugar, candied orange, lemon and citron peel shred with two or three pippins, squeeze in the juice of a lemon, a large glass of sack, with some dates shred small, mix these together, then make your pyes; and when they are served up, strew sugar over them.

To make Mince Pyes the best way.

Take three pounds of suet shred very fine, and chopped as small as possible, two pounds of raisins stoned, and chopped as fine as possible, two pounds of currants nicely picked, washed, rubbed, and dried at the fire, half a hundred of fine pippins, pared, cored and chopped small, half a pound of fine sugar pounded fine, a quarter of an ounce of mace, a quarter of an ounce of cloves, and two large nutmegs, all beat fine; put all together into a great pan, and mix it well together with half a pint of brandy, and half a pint of sweet white wine; put it down close in a stone-
pot,

pot, and it will keep good four months. When you make your pyes, take a little dish, something bigger than a soup-plate, lay a very then crust all over it, lay a thin lare of meat, and then a thin lare of citron cut very thin, then a thin lare of mince-meat, and a thin lare of orange-peel cut thin, over that a little meat, squeeze half the juice of a fine Seville orange or lemon, and pour in three spoonfuls of red wine; lay on your crust, and bake it nicely. These pyes eat finely cold. If you make them in little patties, mix your meat and sweet-meats accordingly. If you chuse meat in your pyes, parboil a neat's tongue, peel it, and chop the meat as fine as possible, and mix with the rest; or two pounds of the inside of a surloin of beef boiled.

To make Lent Mince Pyes.

Take six eggs boiled hard and chopped fine, twelve pippins pared and chopped small, a pound of raisins stoned and chopped fine, a pound of currants picked clean, a spoonful of sugar beat fine, two ounces of citron and candied orange, both cut fine, a quarter of an ounce of mace and cloves, and a nutmeg beat fine, mix all together with a gill of brandy, and a gill of sack. When you make the pye, squeeze in the juice of a seville orange, and a glass of red wine.

To make Mince Pye Meat to keep.

Pare, core, and chop very fine one pound and a half of apples, one pound and a half of beef suet, two pounds of currants washed clean and dried, and one pound and a half of loaf sugar sifted; cut small half a pound of orange and citron

tron peel, a quarter of an ounce of cinnamon, eight cloves, one nutmeg, and a quarter of a pint of French brandy; mix it all well together, put it close down in a pot, and keep it for your use.

A French Pye.

Take a breast or a neck of lamb, cut it in pieces about the bigness of a crown piece, season it with mace, a little pepper and salt; sheet your dish with paste, lay in the lamb with a few oysters, some cocks' stones and combs, and a piece of butter; then close it up, and bake it one hour and a half. Take it out, cut a hole in the top, put in half a pint of cullis, with force-meat balls and made eggs stewed in it, and serve it up for a first course.

To make an Eel Pye.

Skin and clean the eels, season them with a little nutmeg, pepper and salt, cut them in long pieces, and make your pye with good butter-paste; let it be oval, with a thin crust, lay in your eels lengthways, putting over them some fresh butter, then bake them.

To make a Herring Pye.

Scale, gut, and wash them very clean, cut off the heads, fins and tails; make a good crust, cover your dish, then season your herrings with salt, pepper, and beaten mace; put a little butter on the bottom of the dish, then a row of herrings, pare some apples and onions, and cut them in thin slices all over thick, lay a little butter on the top, put in a little water; lay on the lid, and bake it well.

To make a Salmon Pye.

Make a good cruſt, clean your ſalmon well, ſeaſon it with ſalt, mace, and nutmeg; lay a piece of butter at the bottom of your diſh, and lay the ſalmon in; melt butter according to your pye; take a lobſter, boil it, pick out all the fleſh, chop it ſmall, bruiſe the body, mix it well with the butter, which muſt be very good; pour it over the ſalmon, put on the lid and bake it.

To make a Trout Pye.

Clean and ſcale your trout, and lard them with pieces of a ſilver eel rolled up in ſpice, ſweet herbs, and bay leaves powdered; lay between and on them, the bottoms of ſliced artichokes, oyſters, muſhrooms, capers, and ſliced lemon; lay on butter, and cloſe up the pye.

To make an Oyſter Pye.

Firſt parboil a quart of large oyſters, in their own liquor, then mince then ſmall, and pound them in a mortar with marrow, piſtacho-nuts, ſweet herbs, an onion, ſavoury ſpice, and a little grated bread, or ſeaſon them in the ſame manner whole; lay on butter, and cloſe the pye.

To make a Lobſter Pye.

Boil two lobſters, take out the tails, cut them in two, take out the gut, cut each tail in four pieces, and lay them in the diſh. Take the bodies, bruiſe them well with the claws, and pick out the reſt of the meat; chop it all together, ſeaſon it with pepper, ſalt, and two or three ſpoonfuls of vinegar; melt half a pound of butter, ſtir all together, with the crumbs of a

roll

roll rubbed in a cloth small, lay it over the tails, put on your cover, and bake it in a slow oven.

To make a Turbit Pye.

Take some cold boiled turbit, cut it in slices, three inches long and two inches broad, season it with pepper, salt, and nutmeg; two mushrooms, parsley, and thyme shred fine; sheet a dish with light paste, lay in your fish with six ounces of butter and a little gravy; cover it up, ornament it, and bake it three quarters of an hour. Make a force-meat of ten oysters, a few shrimps, and some crumbs of bread; season it with pepper, salt, and mace, chop it fine, and mix it with the yolks of two eggs; make it into balls, and fry them brown in butter, put them in a stew-pan with some gravy, the tail of a lobster cut in dice, one anchovy, a little catchup and lemon juice, thicken it up with a piece of butter and flour, let it just boil. When the pye is baked, take off the lid, pour in the sauce, and serve it up hot for a first course.

To make an Apple Pye.

Scald about a dozen apples very tender, take off the skin, take the core from them, and put to it twelve eggs, but six whites; beat them well, and take the crumbs of a penny loaf, and a nutmeg grated, sugar it to your taste, and put a quarter of a pound of butter in, melted; mix all together in the dish, and take care your oven is not too hot.

To make a Cherry Pye.

Make a good crust, lay a little round the sides

of your dish, throw sugar at the bottom, and lay in your fruit and sugar at top. A few red currants does well with them; put on your lid, and bake it in a slack oven.—Make a plumb and gooseberry pye the same way. If you would have it red, let it stand a while in the oven, after the bread is drawn.

To make a raised Beef Steak Pye.

Beat six rump steaks very well with the rolling-pin, season them with pepper and salt, and three shalots chopt fine; have ready a raised coffin of paste that will just hold them, lay in your steaks, with a quarter of a pound of butter on the top, and half a pint of gravy; close it up, ornament it, bake it two hours, and serve it up for the middle of the table in a first course.

T A R T S.

To make all sorts of Tarts.

IF you bake in tin-patties, butter them, and you must put a little crust all over, because of the taking them out; if in china or glass no crust but the top one. Lay fine sugar at the bottom, then your fruit and sugar at top; then put on your lid, and bake them in a slack oven. Apple, Pear, Apricot, &c. make thus; apples or pears, pare them, cut them in quarters, and core them; cut the quarters across again, set them on in a sauce-pan, with just as much water as will cover them, let them simmer on a slow fire till the fruit is tender, put a good piece of lemon-peel in the water with the fruit, then have your patties ready;

lay

lay sugar at bottom, then your fruit, and a little sugar at top; pour over each tart a tea spoonful of lemon-juice, and three tea spoonfuls of the liquor they were boiled in; put on your lid, and bake them in a slack oven. Do not use lemon to apricots.

As to preserved tarts, only lay in your preserved fruit, and put a thin crust at top, and let them be baked as little as possible; but if you would make them very nice, have a large patty, the size you would have your tart. Make your sugar crust, roll it as thin as a halfpenny, then butter your patties and cover it; shape your upper crust on a hollow thing on purpose, the size of your patty, and mark it with an iron for that purpose, in what shape you please, to be hollow and open to see the fruit through, then bake it crisp; when the crust is cold, very carefully take it out, and fill it with what fruit you please, lay on the lid, and it is done.

A sugar paste for Tarts.

Rub six ounces of butter into one pound of flour, with two ounces of sugar, two yolks of eggs, and a little water or milk; make it into a paste, roll it pretty thin, and sheet your tarts with it; when they are made, bake them in a slow oven; when done, ice them over the top as follows: Beat the white of an egg a little, do it over the top with a pastry-brush, dust on a little fine sugar, then sprinkle on a little water, dust on a little more sugar, set it in the oven for a quarter of an hour to dry, and it will look like ice.

A short paste for Tarts.

Rub a pound of wheat flour, and three quarters of a pound of butter together, put two or three spoonfuls of loaf sugar to it, beat and sifted, the yolks of four eggs beat very well, put to them a spoonful or two of rose-water, and work them all together into a paste, then roll it thin, and ice them over, and bake in a slow oven.

Another paste for Tarts.

Half a pound of butter, half a pound of flour, and half a pound of sugar; mix it well together, beat it, and roll it out thin.

Puff-

Puff-paste.

Take a quarter of a peck of flour, rub fine half a pound of butter, a little salt, make it up into a light paste with cold water, just stiff enough to work it well up; then roll it out, and stick pieces of butter all over, and strew a little flour; roll it up and roll it out again; and so do nine or ten times, till you have rolled in a pound and a half of butter. This crust is mostly used for all sorts of pyes.

Paste for a crackling crust.

Blanch four handfuls of almonds, put them in water, dry them in a cloth, and pound them in a mortar very fine, with a little orange-flour water, and the white of an egg; when they are well pounded, pass them through a coarse hair-sieve, to clear them from lumps; then spread it on a dish till it is very pliable; let it stand a while, then roll out a piece for the under crust, and dry it on the pye-pan in the oven, while other pasty-works are making; as knots, cyphers, &c. for garnishing your pyes.

P U D D I N G S.

Rules *to be observed in making* Puddings.

FOR boiled puddings, let your cloth be kept very clean, dip it in boiling water, rub a little butter on it, and dust with flour; if a batter pudding tie it close; if a bread one, tie it rather loose, and let your water be boiling when put in, and kept so till enough, observing that there be water sufficient to keep it from sticking to the pot; when enough, dip it in cold water, take the upper part of the cloth off, put your dish over it, and with the under part of the cloth turn it carefully out upon your dish. When a batter pudding is made, strain it through a coarse hair sieve, to avoid lumps and treads of eggs; and in all others, strain the eggs when beat. If you boil them in bowls or china-dishes, butter the inside before you put in the batter; and

and for all basted puddings, butter the pan or dish before the pudding is put in. White pot, bread, and custard puddings require a moderate oven; lemon, almond, and orange puddings should have a quicker oven, to raise the paste.

To make Black Puddings.

Put a quarter of a peck of groats into a pot with some new milk, and let them stew till tender; when cold, add a little grated bread, and three pounds of beef suet chopped, one nutmeg, pepper, salt, and mace, season them with thyme, sweet marjoram, (or mint, if you like it) rubbed or chopt very fine; add two quarts of swine or beef blood, mix it all well together, then take the guts and fill them; but be sure the guts are well cleaned, tie them in links, and boil them very carefully. Let them not be too full, or they will burst in boiling.

To make a Marrow Pudding.

Boil a pint of cream, and the marrow of two bones, except a few bits to lay on the top, then slice a penny loaf into it; when it is cold, put to it half a pound of blanched almonds beaten fine, with two spoonfuls of rose-water, the yolks of six eggs, a glass of sweet white wine, a little salt, six ounces of candied citron and lemon sliced thin; mix all these together, then lay on the bits of marrow, bake and serve it up; you may add half a pound of currants. When you boil cream, take care to stir it all the time.

To make a boiled Marrow Pudding.

Pour one pint of boiling cream on the crumbs of a penny loaf, shred three quarters of a pound
of

of beef marrow very thin, add five eggs well beaten, a glass of brandy, sugar and nutmeg to your taste, a quarter of a pound of citron and orange peel, half a pound of currants washed clean, and a quarter of a pound of jar raisins stoned; put it in a cloth, tie it up tight, and boil it an hour and a half; garnish it with slices of orange, and serve it up with melted butter and white wine.

To make a very fine Pudding.

Take a pint of boiled cream, put to it a little nutmeg and mace, then take the crumb of two French rolls and put into the cream, then take the yolks of six eggs, and twenty almonds beaten small, and half a pound of marrow; mingle all together, and season it with a little sugar and salt, and send it to the oven.

To make a very good Plumb Pudding.

Take a quart of milk, twelve ounces of currants, the like quantity of raisins of the sun stoned, a pound and a half of suet chopped small, eight eggs and four whites, half a nutmeg grated, a little beaten ginger, a spoonful of brandy, a few sweetmeats, and mixed up very stiff with flour. Your may bake or boil it.

To make a Light Pudding.

Put some cinnamon, mace, and nutmeg into a pint of cream, and boil it; then take out the spice; take the yolks of eight eggs, and four of the whites, beat them well with some sack, then mix them with the cream, with a little salt and sugar, and take a halfpenny white loaf, and a spoonful of flour, and a little rose-water; beat all well

well together, and wet a thick cloth, and flour it, then put your pudding into it, tie it up, and let it boil an hour. Melt some butter, sack, and sugar, and pour over it.

For making a Bread Pudding.

Put a quarter of a pound of butter into a pint of cream, set it on the fire, and keep stirring it, when the butter is melted, put in as much grated bread as will make it very light, some grated nutmeg, and a little sugar, four eggs, and a little salt; mix all well together, butter the dish, put it in, and bake it half an hour.

To make a Carrot Pudding.

Rasp seven ounces of raw carrot, put to it half a pound of grated bread, pour on it one pint of boiling cream, a little cinnamon and nutmeg, a little brandy, and the yolks of seven eggs; beat it all well together, with six ounces of butter, and sweeten it to your taste; garnish the dish with light paste, put in the pudding, and bake it three quarters of an hour.

To make a Rice Pudding.

Take half a pound of rice, with three pints of new milk, boil it well, when it is almost cold, put to it eight eggs well beaten, and but half whites, with half a pound of butter, and as much sugar as will sweeten it; and some nutmeg or mace. It will take half an hour or more to bake it.

To make a cheap baked Rice Pudding.

Take a quarter of a pound of rice, boil it in a quart of new milk, stir it that it does not burn; when it is thick, take it off, let it stand till it is cool, then stir in a quarter of a pound of butter, and

and sugar to your palate; grate a small nutmeg, butter your dish, pour it in, and bake it.

To make a Batter Pudding.

Take six eggs, a pint of milk, and four spoonfuls of flour, put in a little salt, and half a grated nutmeg; you must take care that your pudding is not too thick, flour your cloth well. Three quarters of an hour will boil it. Serve it with butter, sugar, and a little sweet white wine.

To make a Quaking Pudding.

Beat eight eggs very well, put to them three spoonfuls of fine wheat flour, a pint and a half of cream, a little salt, and boil it with a stick of cinnamon, and a blade of mace; when it is cold, mix it, butter your cloth, but do not give it over much room in the cloth. About an hour will boil it. You must turn it in the boiling or the flour will settle; serve it up with melted butter.

To make a Gooseberry Pudding.

Pick, coddle, bruise, and rub a quart of green gooseberries through a hair sieve to take out the pulp, take six spoonfuls of the pulp, six eggs, half a pound of clarified butter, three quarters of a pound of sugar, some lemon peel shred fine, a handful of bread crumbs, one spoonful of rosewater; mix these well together, and bake it with paste round the dish. You may add sweetmeats.

To make a Custard Pudding.

Beat six eggs in a pint of cream, with two spoonfuls of flour, half a nutmeg grated, a little salt and sugar to your taste; butter a cloth and put it in when the pot boils. Boil it half an hour.

To make a plain Pudding.

You muſt ſcald your milk, and put in as much grated bread as ſuet, and put your milk to it; then cover it a quarter of an hour, ſeaſon it with nutmeg and ginger, and one ſpoonful of ſugar; mix it up well with flour, and boil it two hours.

To make a Carrot Pudding.

Grate two carrots, put in a pint of cream, eight eggs, ſome ſugar, ſack, ſalt and nutmeg, and four ounces of melted butter; mix this well, and cut ſome candied orange and lemon-peel and put in, ſo bake or boil it.

To make a ground Rice Pudding.

Take half a pound of ground rice, half cree it in a quart of milk, when it is cold put to it five eggs well beat, a gill of cream, a little lemon-peel ſhred fine, half a nutmeg grated, half a pound of butter, and half a pound of ſugar; mix all well together, put them into your diſh with a little ſalt, and bake it with a puff-paſte round your diſh; have a little roſe-water, butter and ſugar to pour over it. You may prick in it candied lemon or citron, if you chuſe.—Half of the above quantity will make a pudding for a ſide-diſh.

To make a Hunting Pudding.

Take a pound of fine flour, a pound of beef-ſuet ſhred fine, three quarters of a pound of currants well cleaned, a quartern of raiſins ſtoned and ſhred, five eggs, a little lemon-peel ſhred fine, half a nutmeg grated, a gill of cream, a little ſalt, about two ſpoonfuls of ſugar, and a little brandy;

brandy; mix all well together, and tie it up in a cloth; it will take two hours boiling. You muſt have a little white wine and butter for ſauce.

To make an Orange Pudding.

Take half a pound of grated bread, pour on it one pint of boiled cream or milk, let it ſtand a little, add to it the rind of three Seville oranges boiled tender, and pounded in a mortar;. add the juice of two oranges, the yolks of ſix eggs, a little brandy, nutmeg, and ſugar to your taſte; mix it well together, then butter a cloth to put it in, and boil it three quarters of an hour; when done, take it out, dip it in cold water, put it in a ſieve, turn it carefully into a diſh, and make a ſauce as follows:—Put a little thick melted butter into a ſtew-pan, add to it the juice of one orange, a little ſweet wine and ſugar, let it juſt boil, then pour it over the pudding, and ſerve it up hot.

To make a Lemon Pudding.

Grate the rind of four lemons, put it into a bowl, ſtrain to it the juice, add three quarters of a pound of butter, three quarters of a pound of lump ſugar, the yolks of ten eggs, and the whites of five; mix it all well together, with a little nutmeg, and a tea-cup full of brandy; ſheet a diſh with light paſte, put in the pudding, and bake it three quarters of an hour.

To make an Oxford Pudding.

Take a quarter of a pound of biſcuit grated, a quartern of currants cleaned, a quarter of a pound of ſuet ſhred ſmall, half a ſpoonful of fine ſugar,

a

a very little falt, and fome grated nutmeg: mix all well together, then take the yolks of two eggs, and make it up in balls as big as a turkey's egg. Fry them in frefh butter of a light brown; for fauce have melted butter and fugar, with a little fack or white wine. You muft keep the pan fhaking about, that they may be all of a fine light brown.

To make a Sagoe Pudding.

Let half a pound of fagoe be wafhed well in three or four waters, then put to it a quart of new milk, and boil it till it is thick, ftir it carefully, (for it is apt to burn) put in a ftick of cinnamon, when it is boiled take it out; before you pour it out, ftir in half a pound of frefh butter, then pour it into a pan, and beat up nine eggs, with five of the whites, and four fpoonfuls of fack; ftir all together, and fweeten to your tafte. Put in a quarter of a pound of currants clean wafhed and rubbed, and juft plumped in two fpoonfuls of fack and two of rofe-water; mix all together, lay a puff-pafte over a difh, pour in the ingredients, and bake it.

To make a Potatoe Pudding.

Boil your large potatoes as you would do for eating, beat them with a little rofe water, and a glafs of fack, put to them half a pound of melted butter, the like quantity of currants well cleaned, a little fhred lemon-peel and candied orange; mix all together, bake and ferve it up.

To make a Calf's Foot Pudding.

Take a pound of calves feet minced fine, the fat

fat and the brown to be taken out, a pound and a half of fuet, pick off the skin and shred it small, six eggs, but half the whites, beat them well, the crumb of a halfpenny roll grated, a pound of currants cleaned, milk as much as will moisten it with the eggs, a handful of flour, a little salt, nutmeg, and sugar, to season it to your taste; boil it nine hours with your meat. When it is done, lay it in your dish, and pour melted butter over it. It is good with white wine and sugar in the butter.

A boiled Suet Pudding.

Take a quart of milk, a pound of suet shred small, four eggs, two spoonfuls of beaten ginger, or one of beaten pepper, a tea-spoonful of salt; mix the eggs and flour with a pint of the milk very thick, and with the seasoning mix in the rest of the milk and the suet; let your batter be very thick, and boil it two hours.

To make a White Pot Pudding.

Cut half a pound of biscuit cake into thin slices, and lay it in a china dish; boil a quart of cream, with a few coriander seeds, a little cinnamon, and lemon peel; take it off, and let it cool, add seven eggs, as much sugar as will sweeten it, with a little nutmeg, then strain it into the dish. Three quarters of an hour will bake it. You may garnish the brim of the dish with light paste, if you chuse it.

To make White Puddings in skins.

Blanch one pound of rice in boiling water, drain it upon a sieve, put it into one quart of new

new milk, and boil it till it is soft; add to it one pound of clean washed currants, one pound of beef marrow or hog's lard cut very fine, five eggs, a little mace and cinnamon pounded, and a little salt; mix them all well together, fill your skins lightly, and boil them half an hour very slowly. When you use them, broil them on a gridiron.

To make a Biscuit Pudding.

Grate half a pound of biscuit cake, pour on it one pint of boiling cream; when it is cold, add to it the yolks of six eggs, a little brandy, and half a nutmeg grated; mix it, then butter a cloth or bason, put it in, tie it up tight, and boil it three quarters of an hour. When done, dish it up, garnish it with currant jelly and serve it up with wine sauce in a boat.

To make a Pease Pudding.

Boil it till it is quite tender, then take it up, untie it, stir in a good piece of butter, a little salt, and a good deal of beaten pepper, then tie it up tight again, boil it an hour longer, and it will eat fine.

To make Furmenty.

Take a quart of ready boiled wheat, two quarts of milk, a quarter of a pound of currants clean picked and washed; stir these together and boil them, beat up the yolks of three or four eggs, a little nutmeg, and add two or three spoonfuls of milk to the wheat, stir all together for a few minutes, sweeten to your palate, and send it to table.

To make Plumb Porridge, or Barley Gruel.

Take a gallon of water, half a pound of barley, half a pound of raisins and currants clean washed and picked; boil these till above half the water is wasted, with two or three blades of mace; then sweeten it, and add half a pint of wine.

To make a Sack Posset.

Take a quart of new milk, four Naples biscuits crumbled, and when the milk boils throw them in; just give it a boil, take it off, grate in some nutmeg, and sweeten to your palate; then pour in half a pint of sack, stirring it all the time, and serve it up.

DUMPLINGS.

To make Suet Dumplings.

TAKE a pint of milk, four eggs, a pound of suet, a pound of currants, two tea-spoonfuls of salt, and three of ginger; first take half the milk, and mix it like a thick batter, then put the eggs, and the salt and ginger, then the rest of the milk by degrees, with the suet and currants, and flour to make it like a light paste; when the water boils make them in rolls as big as a turkey's egg, with a little flour; then flat them, throw them into boiling water, and move them softly, that they don't stick together, keep the water boiling all the time, and half an hour will boil them.

To make Yeast Dumplings

First make a light dough as for bread, with flour,

flour, water, salt and yeast, cover it with a cloth, and set it before the fire for half an hour, then have a sauce-pan of water on the fire; and when it boils take the dough, and make it into round balls; flat them with your hand, and put them in the water, ten minutes boil them; take great care they don't fall to the bottom, for they will be heavy; and be sure to keep the water boiling all the time. When they are enough, take them up, lay them in your dish, and have melted butter in a cup.

To make hard Dumplings.

Rub into your flour a good piece of butter, then make it like a crust for a pye; make them up, have the water boiling, throw them in, and half an hour will boil them. They are best boiled with a piece of beef. Have butter in a cup.

To make hard Dumplings another way.

Mix flour and water with some salt, like a paste, roll them in balls, as big as a turkey's egg, roll them in a little flour, and boil them as before.

To make Norfolk Dumplings.

Mix a good thick batter, as for pancakes; take half a pint of milk, two eggs, a little salt, and make it into a batter with flour; have ready a clean sauce-pan of water boiling, into which drop this batter; be sure the water boils fast, and two or three minutes will boil them; then throw them into a sieve to drain, turn them into a dish, and stir a lump of fresh butter in them; eat them hot, and they are very good.

To

To make Apple Dumplings.

Make a good puff-paste, pare some large apples, cut them in quarters, and take out the cores very nicely, take a piece of crust and roll it round, enough for one apple; if they are big they will not look pretty; so roll the crust round each apple, and make them round like a ball, with a little flour in your hand; have a pot of water boiling, take a clean cloth, dip it in the water, and shake flour over it; tie each dumpling by itself, and put them in the water boiling, which keep boiling all the time; and if your crust is light and good, and the apples not too large, half an hour will boil them; but if the apples be large, they will take an hour boiling. When they are enough, take them up, lay them in a dish, throw fine sugar all over them, and send them to table. Have good fresh butter melted in a cup, and fine sugar in a saucer.

Directions for making BROTHS, SOOPS, GRAVIES, &c.

Rules to be observed in making Soups or Broths.

FIRST take great care the pots or sauce-pans and covers be very clean and free from all grease and sand, and that they be well tinned, for fear of giving the broths and soups any brassy taste. If you have time to stew as softly as you can, it will both have a finer flavour, and the meat will be tenderer. But then observe, when you make soups or broths for present use, if it is to be done softly, don't put much more water than you intend to have soup or broth; and if you have the convenience of an earthen pan or pipkin, set it on wood embers till it boils, then skim it, and put in your seasoning; cover it close, and set it on embers, so that it may do very softly for some time, and both

both the meat and broths will be delicious. You must observe in all broths and soups that one thing does not taste more than another; but that the taste be equal, and it has a fine agreeable relish, according to what you design it for; and you must be sure, that all the greens and herbs you put in be cleaned, washed, and picked.

To make Broths for Soops or Gravy.

Chop a leg of beef to pieces, set it on the fire in about four gallons of water, scum it very clean, season it with white pepper, a few cloves, and a bunch of sweet herbs; boil it till two thirds is wasted, then season it with salt; let it boil a little while longer, then you may strain it off, and keep it for use.

Beef Broth.

Crack the bone of a leg of beef in two or three parts, put it in a gallon of water, then put in two or three blades of mace, a crust of bread, salt, and a bunch of parsley. Boil it till the beef and sinews are tender; cut some toasted bread in square pieces, and lay it in your dish. Lay in the meat, and pour your soop over it.

Jelly Broth for Consumptive Persons.

Take a joint of mutton, a capon, a fillet of veal, and five quarts of water, put these in an earthen pot, boil them over a gentle fire till one half be consumed; then squeeze altogether, and strain the liquor through a linen cloth.

Pork Broth for weak People.

Take two pounds of young pork; then take off the skin and fat, boil it in a gallon of water, with a turnip and a very little corn of salt. Let it boil till it comes to two quarts, then strain it off, and let it stand till cold. Take off the fat, then leave the settling at the bottom of the pan, and drink half a pint in the morning fasting, an hour before breakfast; and at noon, if the stomach will bear it.

To make Beef or Mutton Broth for very weak people.

Take a pound of beef or mutton, or both together, to a pound put two quarts of water, firſt ſkin the meat and take off all the fat; then cut it into ſmall pieces, and boil it till it comes to a quarter of a pint. Seaſon it with a very little corn of ſalt, ſkim off all the fat, and give a ſpoonful of this broth at a time. To very weak people, half a ſpoonful is enough; to ſome a tea ſpoonful at a time; and to others a tea-cup full. There is greater nouriſhment from this than any thing elſe.

To make Chicken Broth.

Skin a ſmall chicken, cut it in four pieces, put it in a ſtew-pan with one quart of water, two or three blades of mace, a few white pepper corns, and a ſmall cruſt of bread, ſet it on the fire to boil, ſkim it clean, let it boil gently for three quarters of an hour, ſtrain it, and ſerve it up in a baſon, with a dry toaſt.

To make Chicken Water.

Skin a ſmall chicken, break the bones, and cut it very ſmall and thin, put it into a ſtone jar, pour on it a pint and a half of boiling water, cover it cloſe, ſet it before the fire for four hours, then ſtrain and uſe it.

To make Beef Tea.

Cut three quarters of a pound of lean beef into thin ſlices, put it into a large tea-pot, and pour on it one pint and a half of boiling water, ſtop it cloſe, ſet it before the fire for two hours, and then uſe it.

To make Travelling Mutton Broth.

You muſt have one neck and one loin of mutton, cut them into ſix pieces each joint; then waſh it from the blood; then put in as much water as will cover it; ſeaſon with pepper, ſalt, a faggot of herbs, cloves and mace; then put in two or three ſlit onions, and a few marigolds When it is boiled one hour and a half, ſkim off the fat, and put in ſome ſlices of toaſted bread, and diſh up your chops in the middle of your diſh.

SOOPS.

SOOPS.

To make a fine White Soop.

TAKE a leg of beef, and a knuckle of veal, and let them boil at least four hours, then beat a pound of sweet almonds very fine, and mix them with some of the broth, and then strain off the rest from the meat, and serve it with the almonds in it, with sippets of fried bread.

To make solid or portable Soop.

Get a leg of veal, or any other young meat, cut off the fat, and make a strong broth after the common way; put this into a wide bason, or a stew-pan well tinned; let it stew gently over a slow fire till it is boiled away to one third of the quantity, then take it from the fire, and set over water that is kept constantly boiling, this being an even heat and not apt to burn to the vessel; in this manner let it evaporate, stirring it often till it becomes, when cold, as hard a substance as glue; then let it dry by a gentle warmth and keep it from moisture. When you use it, pour boiling water upon it. It makes excellent broth, either strong or small according to the quantity you put in. It will keep good at least twelve months.

To make Peas Soop.

Make two quarts of good broth from beef and pickled pork; take cellery, turnip, onion, mint, and all sorts of kitchen herbs, stew them down tender with a piece of butter; rub all these through a sieve; and one pint of peas being boiled to a pulp, rub them through a sieve, thinning it with your broth, till all is through. Season it with pepper and salt, and have boiled tender some cellery and leek cut small to put in the soop. White peas and green peas are both done this way. Fry some bread to put in it.

To make a Gravy Soop.

Cut a pound of mutton, a pound of veal, and a pound of beef in little pieces; put it into seven quarts of water, with an old fowl beat to pieces, an onion, a carrot, some white pepper and salt, a little bunch of sweet herbs, two blades of mace, a few cloves, some cellery, cabbage, endive, turnips, and lettice; let it stew over a slow fire till half is wasted, then strain it off for use.

To make a good stock for Soops of Flesh.

Take a piece of brisket beef, a neck of mutton, a knuckle of veal, and a fowl; wash them and put them in your pot, which fill up with soft water, and when it boils, skim it clean; then season it with a faggot of herbs, whole pepper, salt, cloves and mace, and put in a crust of bread; boil all very well, but take out your fowl and knuckle of veal before they are boiled to rags; strain all for use.

To make a Calf's Head Soop.

Stew a calf's head tender, then strain off the liquor, and put into it a bunch of sweet herbs, onion, mace, some pearl barley, pepper and salt, boil all a small time, and serve up with the head in the middle, boned. Garnish with bread toasted brown, and grated round the rim.

To make Hare Soop.

Cut the hare in pieces, wash it and put it into a stew-pan, with a knuckle of veal, put in it a gallon of water, a little salt, and a handful of sweet herbs; let it stew till the gravy be good; fry a little of the hare to brown the soop. You may put in it some crust of white bread among the mace to thicken the soop: put it into a dish, with a little stewed spinage, crisped bread, and a few forced-meat balls. Garnish your dish with boiled spinage and turnips, cut it in thin slices.

To make Veal Soop.

Take a knuckle of veal, cut it in pieces, boil with it a pullet and half a pound of almonds beat small, stove it well and very tender, (you may boil a chicken to lay in the middle) then skim it clean, and season it with salt and a blade of mace, then take the yolks of four eggs and beat them up in a little cool broth, draw it up thickish as cream, and serve it away hot.

To make Oyster Soop.

Your stock must be of fish, then take two quarts of oysters, set and beard them, take the hard part of the oysters from the other, beat them in a mortar with ten hard yolks of eggs, put in some good stock, season it with pepper, salt, and nutmeg, then thicken up your soop as cream, put in the rest of your oysters, and garnish with oysters.

Onion Soop.

Take four or five large onions, peel and boil them in milk and water whilst tender, (shifting them two or three times in the boiling) beat them in a marble mortar to a pulp, and rub them through a hair sieve, and put them into a little sweet gravy, then fry a few slices of bacon; beat them in a marble mortar as small as forced meat; put it into your stew-pan with the gravy and onions, and boil them; mix a spoonful of wheat flour, with a little water favoury, and put it into the soop to keep it from running; strain all through a cullendar, season it to your taste, then put into the dish a little spinage stewed in butter, and a little crisp bread, so serve it up.

To make Peas Soop in Lent.

Take a quart of peas, put them into a pot with a gallon of water, two or three large onions, six anchovies, a little whole pepper and salt; boil all together whilst your soop is thick, strain it into a stew-pan through your cullendar, and put six ounces of butter

(worked

(worked in flour) into the foop to thicken it; alfo put in a little boiled celery, ftewed fpinage, crifp bread, and a little dried mint powdered; fo ferve it up.

To make Soop Meagre for Lent.

Take fix heads of cellery, fix large onions, three carrots, three parfnips, and three turnips, cut them into flices, and put them into a ftew-pan with fix ounces of butter, and a pint of fplit peas, let them ftew for a quarter of an hour, then put in two quarts of boiling water, let them ftew flowly till the peas are quite tender, then work them through a fieve with a wooden fpoon, into a ftew-pan; have ready three heads of cellery, three cabbage lettices, fix leaves of fpinage, fhred them all very fine, and fry them in butter, put them into your foop with a little dried mint rubbed fine, let them fimmer for a quarter of an hour, add pepper and falt to your tafte, and ferve it up with fried bread.

A common Peas Soop in Winter.

Put a quart of good boiling peas into a gallon of foft cold water, add thereto a little beef or mutton, and a little bacon, with an onion or two, boil all together till it is thick, falt it to your tafte and thicken it with wheat flour, ftrain it through a cullendar, boil fome celery, cut it in pieces, with fome crifp bread, and crifp fome fpinage as you would do parfley, then put it in a difh, and garnifh with rafpings of bread.

To make Rice Soop.

Your ftock muft be of veal and fowl, put in half a pound of rice, a pint of good gravy and a knuckle of veal, ftove it tender; feafon it with mace and falt, then make a rim round your difh, and garnifh your difh with heaps of rice, fome coloured with faffron, placing one heap of white and one yellow all round.

To make an Almond Soop.

Take a quart of almonds, blanch them, and beat them in a marble mortar, with the yolks of twelve hard eggs, till they are a fine paste; mix them by degrees with two quarts of new milk, a quart of cream, a quarter of a pound of double refined sugar, beat fine, a pennyworth of orange-flour water, stir all well together; when it is well mixed, set it over a slow fire, and keep it stirring quick all the while, till you find it is thick enough, then pour it in your dish and send it to table. If you don't be very careful it will curdle.

To make Vermegelly Soop.

Boil six ounces of vermegelly in water for a quarter of an hour, and strain it through a sieve; put two quarts of broth into a stew-pan, and a fowl trussed as for boiling, let it simmer for one hour, then put in the vermegelly, let it simmer a little, put your fowl into a turreen, pour your soop over it, and serve it up.

GRAVIES.

To make good Gravy.

LAY some slices of ham or bacon at the bottom of your gravy, put in some pieces of beef pretty thick, then lay on slices of onion and celery, or leeks, and a little parsley and thyme; stove it gently till it comes to a brown, then put in some good broth, and you may have it what colour you please. Strain it off for use.

Gravy for White Sauce.

Cut a pound of veal into small pieces, boil it in about a quart of water, with a blade of mace, an onion, some white pepper, and two cloves; let it boil till it is of a proper strength.

Gravy for Turkey, Fowl, or Ragoo.

Take a pound of lean beef, cut, and hack it well, then flour it well, put a piece of butter as big as a hen's hen's egg in a stew-pan; when it is melted put in your beef, fry it on all sides a little brown, then pour in three pints of boiling water, and a bundle of sweet herbs, two or three blades of mace, three or four cloves, twelve whole pepper-corns, a little bit of carrot, a little piece of crust of bread toasted brown; cover it close, and let it boil till there is about a pint or less; then season it with salt, and strain it off.

To make good and cheap Gravy.

Take twelve penny-worth of coarse lean beef, cut it in pieces, flour it well, take a quarter of a pound of good butter, put it into a little pot or large deep stew pan, and put in your beef; keep stirring it, and when it looks a little brown, pour in a pint of boiling water, stir it all together, put in a large onion, a bundle of sweet herbs, two or three blades of mace, six cloves, a spoonful of whole pepper, a crust of bread toasted, and a bit of carrot, then pour in a gallon of water, stir all together, cover close, and let it stew till it is as rich as you would have it; when enough, strain it off, mix it with two or three spoonfuls of catchup, and a gill of white wine; then put all the ingredients together again, and put in two quarts of boiling water, cover it close, and let it boil till there is about a pint, strain it off well, add it to the first, and give it a boil together. This will make a great deal of rich good gravy.

Gravy for a Fowl, when you have no meat or gravy ready.

Take the neck, liver, and gizzard, boil them in half a pint of water, with a little piece of bread toasted brown, a little pepper and salt, and a little thyme; let them boil to a quarter of a pint, then pour in half a glass of red wine, boil it and strain it, then bruise the liver well in, and strain it again, thicken it with a piece of butter rolled in flour, and it will be very good.

A good Gravy for any use.

Take two ounces of butter, and burn it in a frying-pan

pan till it is brown, then put in two pounds of coarse lean beef, two quarts of water, half a pint of red or white wine, as you would have the colour, four shalots, six mushrooms, cloves, mace, whole pepper, and four anchovies; let it stew an hour over a slow fire, and strain it off for use.

To draw Mutton, Beef, or Veal Gravy.

Take a pound of meat, cut it thin, lay a piece of bacon about two inches long, at the bottom of the pan, and lay the meat on it; lay in some carrot, cover it close for two or three minutes, then pour in a quart of boiling water, some spice, onion, sweet herbs, and a crust of bread toasted; let it stew over a slow fire, and thicken it with a piece of butter rolled in flour, season it with salt, and strain it off. Leave out the bacon, if you dislike it.

Of COLLARING.

To collar Beef.

TAKE a thin flank of beef, slit it through the middle, salt it with a quarter of a pound of salt-petre, half a pint of petre-salt, and a quart of white salt; let it lie a week, then season it with an ounce of pepper, half an ounce of cloves and mace, a little thyme and lemon-peel shred fine; roll it up tight, bind it hard with coarse tape, and cover it with pump water, then bake it in a pan with houshold bread, and when it comes out of the oven roll it tight in a coarse cloth, and tie it right at both ends; when it is cold, take off the cloth and tape, and keep it in a cool place.

To collar a Breast of Veal, or a Pig.

Bone the pig or veal, then season it in the inside with cloves, mace, and salt beat fine, a handful of sweet herbs stripped off the stalks, and a little pennyroyal and parsley shred fine, with a little sage; then roll it up as you do brawn, bind it with narrow tape very close, tie a cloth round it, and boil it very tender

der in vinegar and water; a like quantity, with a little cloves, mace, pepper, and falt, all whole; make it boil, put in the collars, when boiled tender take them up, and when both are cold take off the cloth, lay the collar in an earthen pan, and pour the liquor over; cover it clofe, and keep it for ufe. If the pickle begins to fpoil, ftrain it through a coarfe cloth, boil it and fkim it, when cold, pour it over. Obferve before you ftrain the pickle, to wafh the collar, wipe it dry, and wipe the pan clean, ftrain it again after it is boiled, and cover it very clofe.

To collar a Breaft of Mutton.

Take a large breaft of mutton, bone it, feafon it with pepper, falt and fpice, thyme and lemon-peel fhred fine, roll it up tight, and bind it hard with tape; boil it two hours in water and falt, with fome whole fpice and pepper, and a bunch of fweet herbs. Serve it in flices with all forts of pickles.

To collar Pork.

Take a belly-piece of pork, bone it, and feafon it high with pepper, falt, fpice, and a good handful of fage fhred; roll it tight as before directed; boil it five hours in the fame pickle as for the veal before. Serve it with muftard and fugar.

To collar a Calf's Head.

Take a calf's head with the fkin on, fcald off the hair, rip it down the face, take out the bones from the meat, fteep it in warm milk and water to make it white, rub it with the white of an egg, and feafon it with white pepper, falt, mace, and nutmeg; fhred fome parfley and thyme very fine, lay it all over the head; cut off the ears, lay them on the thin part of the head, roll it up tight, tie it in a cloth, then boil it one hour and a half in foft water and a little milk, to keep it white; when done, tie it up tight as before. When it is cold, put it in a pickle, the fame as for brawn, and ferve it up in flices.

To collar Eels.

Take a large eel, and split it down the back; take out the bone, season it high with pepper, salt and spice, and a little thyme shred fine; roll it up into a collar, put a cloth about it, and bind it with tape; boil it an hour in white wine vinegar, of each a like quantity, with whole pepper and spice, and a bunch of sweet herbs, a slice or two of lemon, with a little salt. When it is cold, take off the tape and the cloth, and keep it in the pickle you boil it in. Serve it in slices, with oil, lemon, and some of the pickle.

To collar Salmon.

Take a side of salmon, cut off about a handful of the tail, wash your large piece very well, and dry it with a cloth, then wash it over with the yolks of eggs, then make some force-meat with that you cut off the tail, but take care of the skin, and put to it a handful of parboiled oysters, a tail or two of lobster, the yolks of three or four eggs boiled hard, six anchovies, a handful of sweet herbs shred small, a little salt, pepper, cloves, mace, and nutmeg, all beat fine, with grated bread; work all these together into a body, with the yolks of eggs, lay it all over the fleshy part, and a little more pepper and salt over the salmon, to roll it up into a collar, and bind it with broad tape, then boil it in water, salt, and vinegar, but let the liquor boil first, then put in your collar a bunch of sweet herbs, sliced ginger, and nutmeg; let it boil two hours gently, and when it is enough, take it up, put it into your sousing pan, and when the pickle is cold put it to your salmon, and let it stand in it till used; or you may pot it. After it is boiled, pour clarified butter over it. It will keep longest so, but either way is good. If you pot it, be sure the butter be very good.

Of RAGOOS.

To ragoo Lamb Stones.

HAVING got two or three pair of lamb ſtones, parboil them, take off the ſkin, cut them in four or eight pieces, ſtrew ſome ſalt over them, and wipe them dry; flour, but don't touch them with your hands, fry them immediately with very hot hog's lard, and make them criſp, then diſh them up, and ſerve away.

To ragoo Lamb.

Cut a breaſt and neck of lamb into four pieces each, ſeaſon them well with beaten cloves, mace, pepper, and ſalt, put them into a ſtew-pan with a piece of butter, fry them brown, and duſt in ſome flour, add a pint and a half of gravy, a bunch of ſweet herbs, a few morels and muſhrooms, two ſpoonfuls of red wine, and a little juice of lemon, let it ſtew till tender, skim off the fat, then add one dozen of fried forcemeat balls, let it juſt ſimmer, and ſerve it up hot for a firſt courſe.

To ragoo a Leg of Mutton.

Take off the fat and ſkin, cut it very thin the right way of the grain, then butter your ſtew-pan, and ſhake ſome flour into it; ſlice half a lemon and half an onion, cut them very ſmall, a little bundle of ſweet herbs, and a blade of mace; put all together with your meat into the pan, ſtir it a minute or two, then put in ſix ſpoonfuls of gravy, and have ready an anchovy mixed ſmall; mix it with ſome butter and flour, ſtir all together for ſix minutes, and then diſh it up.

To ragoo a Neck of Veal.

Cut it in ſteaks, flatten them with a rolling-pin, ſeaſon them with ſalt, pepper, cloves, and mace, lard them with bacon, lemon-peel, and thyme, dip them in the yolks of eggs, make a ſheet of ſtrong paper up at the four corners in the form of a dripping-pan,

pan, pin up the corners, butter the paper and gridiron, and set it over a fire of charcoal; put in your meat, let it do gently, keep it basting and turning to keep in the gravy; and, when it is enough, have ready half a pint of strong gravy, season it high, put in mushrooms and pickles, force-meat balls dipped in the yolks of eggs, oysters stewed and fried, to lay round and at the top of your dish, and then serve it up. If for a brown ragoo, put in red wine; if for a white one, put in white white, with the yolks of eggs beat up with two or three spoonfuls of cream.

To ragoo a Breast of Veal.

Lard and half roast it, then pour strong gravy upon it, and stew it very well with a bunch of sweet herbs, an onion, pepper, salt, cloves, and mace; for sauce take some butter and brown it, shake some flour into it, take the liquor you stewed your veal in, and boil it with palates, mushrooms, oysters, forced-meat, sweet-breads, and artichoke bottoms; squeeze in a lemon, and after you have strain'd off your herbs, toss it up all together, and pour it over the veal.

To ragoo a Rump of Beef.

Take a rump of beef, lard it with bacon and spices, betwixt the larding stuff it with forced meat, made of a pound of veal, three quarters of a pound of beef suet, a quarter of a pound of fat bacon boiled and shred well by itself, a good deal of parsley, winter-savoury, thyme, sweet-marjoram, and an onion, mix all this together, season it with mace, cloves, cinnamon, salt, Jamaica and black pepper, and some grated bread; work the forced meat up with three whites and two yolks of eggs, then stuff it, and lay some ruff suet in a stew-pan with your beef upon it; let it fry till it is brown, then put in some water, a bunch of sweet-herbs, a large onion stuffed with cloves, sliced turnips, a carrot cut large, some whole pepper and salt, and half a pint of claret; cover it close, and let it stew six or seven hours over a gentle fire, turning it often. For sauce take truffles, morels, sweet-breads,

diced

diced palates boiled tender, three anchovies, and some lemon-peel, put these into some brown gravy and stew them; if is not thick enough, dridge in a little flour, and just before you pour it on your beef put in a little white wine and vinegar, and serve it up hot.

To ragoo a Calf's Head.

Take two calves heads, boil them as you do for eating, when they are cold cut off all the lantern part from the flesh, in pieces about an inch long, and about the breadth of your finger; put it into a stew-pan with a little white gravy, twenty oysters cut in two or three pieces, a few shred mushrooms, and a little juice of lemon; season it with shred mace and salt, let them all boil together over a stove; take two or three spoonfuls of cream, the yolks of three eggs, and a little shred parsley, then put it into a stew-pan; after you have put in the cream, shake it all the while, if you let it boil it will curdle, so serve it up. Garnish your dish with sippets, lemon, and a few pickled mushrooms.

To ragoo Cocks-combs, Cocks-kidneys, and fat Livers.

Take a stew-pan, put in a bit of butter, a bunch of sweet herbs, some mushrooms and truffles; put it for a minute over a fire, flour it a little, moisten it with half a spoonful of broth, season it with salt and pepper; let it stew a little, then put in some cocks-combs, cocks-kidneys, fat livers, and sweet-breads; let your ragoo be palatable, thicken it with the yolks of eggs; serve it up hot for a dainty dish.

A ragoo of Oysters.

Open your large oysters, take them out of their liquor, save the liquor, and dip the oysters in a batter made thus; take two eggs, beat them well, grate a little lemon peel and some nutmeg, a blade of mace pounded fine, a little parsley chopped fine; beat all together with a little flour, have ready some butter or dripping in a stew-pan; when it boils dip in your oysters one by one into the batter, and fry them of a fine brown; then with an egg-slice take them out, and
lay

lay them in a dish before the fire; pour the fat out of the pan, and shake a little flour over the bottom of the pan, then rub a piece of butter as big as a small walnut all over with your knife, whilst it is over the fire; then pour in three spoonfuls of the oyster liquor strained, one spoonful of white wine and a quarter of a pint of gravy; grate some nutmeg, stir all together, throw in the oysters, give the pan a toss round, and when the sauce is of a good thickness, pour all into the dish, and garnish with raspings.

A ragoo of Mushrooms.

Pick small mushrooms, wash and dry them, put them in a stew-pan with a bunch of sweet herbs, season them with pepper, salt, and mace, set them over the fire for four or five minutes, stirring them all the time; moisten them with a little gravy, let them stew gently for half an hour, take out the bunch of herbs, skim of the fat, thicken them up with a little butter and flour, and put the crust of a French roll in the middle of the dish, pour the mushrooms round it, and serve it up hot.—This is a pretty second course dish.

To make a ragoo of Onions.

Take a pint of little young onions, peel them, and take four large ones, peel them and cut them very small; put a quarter of a pound of good butter into a stew-pan, when it is melted and done making a noise, throw in your onions, and fry them till they look brownish; then shake in some flour, and stir them round until they are thick; throw in some salt, beaten pepper, half a gill of good gravy, and a tea-spoonful of mustard: stir all together, and when it is well tasted and of a good thickness pour it into your dish, and garnish it with fried crumbs of bread and raspings. They make a pretty dish, and are very good. You may stew raspings in the room of flour, if you please.

To ragoo Asparagus Heads.

Cut some heads of asparagus in small lengths as far as they are tender, blanch them in some boiling water, and drain them, put them in a stew-pan with some

gravy

gravy and a flice of a ham, feafon them with pepper, falt, and nutmeg, and let them ftew gently till tender; take out the ham, and thicken it up with butter and flour, adding a tea fpoonful of vinegar; put your afparagus into a difh, and garnifh it with fried bread, and ferve it up hot for a fecond courfe difh.

Of POTTING.

To pot Beef.

TAKE a leg of mutton of twelve pounds, and cut it into pound pieces, falt it as for a collar of beef, let it lie fix days, bake it in a pan covered with pump water, and bake it with houfhold bread; when it comes out of the oven, take it out of the liquor, beat it in a ftone mortar; then feafon it with an ounce of pepper, and half an ounce of cloves and mace; mix to it a pound of clarified butter, put it clofe into your pot, and cover it with clarified butter on the top half an inch thick.

To pot a Hare.

Bone your hare and take away all the fkinny part, then put to the flefh fome good fat bacon, and favoury herbs, feafon it with mace, nutmeg, pepper, and fome falt, then beat all this fine in a mortar, then put it down, and bake it about an hour and a half; and when it comes out, pour out all the gravy, and fill it up with clarified butter.

To pot Tongues.

Take two tongues, falt them with falt-petre, white falt, brown fugar, and bake them tender in pump water; then blanch them, and cut off the roots, feafon with pepper and fpice. Put them in an oval pot, and cover them all over with clarified butter.

To pot Salmon.

Take the fkin of two pounds of falmon, feafon it with pepper, falt, mace, and cloves; add a little falt-petre pounded, put it in a pot with a pound of butter over it, and bake it; when it is baked, pick

the

the bones out, and fhred it, add a little of the butter it was baked in, put it down in a pot, and cover it over with the butter in which it was baked.

To pot Lobster.

Boil four lobfters fifteen minutes, take out the meat as whole as you can, feafon it with pepper, falt, mace, and nutmeg; put it into a pot with a pound of butter over it, and fome of the fpawn pounded, to colour the butter; tie a paper over the pot, and bake it half an hour, then take out the meat, and put it clofe down in your potting pot; when it is cold, take the butter in which they were baked clean from the gravy, warm it, and pour it over the lobfter: If this is not enough, clarify a little more, for it muft be covered well with butter.

To pot Lamprey.

Skin and gut them very clean, feafon them with pepper, falt, mace, and nutmeg; lay them in a pot with fome butter, and bake them till tender; take them out, put them in a potting pot, pour the butter over them, and, when cold, cover them with paper.

To pot Eels.

Skin and gut fome large eels, wipe them dry with a cloth, feafon them with pepper, falt, mace, and nutmeg; put them in a pot with their backs downwards; cover them with butter, tie them down with paper, and bake them three quarters of an hour in a moderate oven; when done, take them carefully out with a flice, lay them on a plate to cool, put them into the pots with their backs downward, and pour over them the butter they were baked in. When you ferve them up, dip your pot in hot water, turn them out on a difh, and garnifh them with parfley.

To pot Pigeons.

Pick, clean, and draw the pigeons, trufs them as for boiling, feafon them with pepper, falt, mace, and cloves; put them in a pot, cover them with butter, tie them down with paper, and bake them 'till tender;

take them out, lay them in a plate to cool, then put them in the potting pots, and pour the butter over them.

To pot Moor Game.

Pick and draw three moor game, make them very clean, tuck in their legs, feafon them with pepper, falt, mace, cloves, and nutmeg beaten very fine, and mixed well together; make them pretty high with the feafoning, and put them into a mug that will juft hold them, with two pounds of butter over them; tie a paper over the mug, and fet it into an oven to bake 'till they are tender, but not too much done; then take them out of the butter, let them cool, and put each into a potting pot that will juft hold them, fill the pots up with the butter in which they were baked; if it is not enough, clarify fome more, and fill them up.

To pot Woodcocks.

When they are clean picked, take out the gizzards, but not the trail, (for that is the beft); feafon them with mace, nutmeg, pepper, and falt; lay them in a pot with as much butter as will cover them, bake them three quarters of an hour, then take them out, and put them into pots that will juft hold them; cover them over with the butter in which they were baked; if this is not enough, clarify fome more, and fill them up.

To pot Ham and Fowl.

Chop a piece of cold boiled ham fine, beat it in a mortar, with fome pepper, mace, nutmeg, and a little clarified butter; put a little of it into a glafs bowl; then beat fine the breaft of a fowl, feafon it a little as above; then lay fome fowl into the glafs, then a layer of ham, and fo on of each alternately till the glafs is filled; prefs it tight down, and pour clarified butter over it.

To pot Venifon.

Bone a piece of venifon, feafon it well with pepper, falt, mace, and nutmeg; put it in a pot, with as much butter as will cover it; tie it over with brown paper,

paper, and bake it till tender in a moderate oven; when done, take it out of the gravy, let it cool; pick out the skins and sinews, shred it fine, and pound it in a mortar, then take the butter clean from the gravy it was baked in, and put amongst it: If it is not high enough seasoned, add more, put it in a pot, and cover it with clarified butter. Hare is potted the same way.

To pot Veal.

Cut a piece of a fillet veal, season it pretty high with pepper, salt, mace, and nutmeg; put it into a pot with some butter over it, and bake it till it is tender; take it out of the gravy, shred it, put it in a mortar with some of the butter it was baked in, and pound it till it is like a paste; take it out of the mortar, lay it on a plate, then take some boiled tongue or ham, chop it fine, and pound it in a mortar with a little of the butter the veal was baked in: Lay some of the veal in the bottom of the pot, and some ham or tongue in lumps over it, then a layer of each till the pot is full; press it down, and cover it with clarified butter. When you serve it up, cut it in slices, and garnish it with parsley.

☞ In potting you must observe always *to season well*, and cover every thing with butter, as well as tie down with paper; bake till tender, take it out of the butter, and lay your pot on a cool dish. If beef, veal, or hare, pick out the strings and sinews before you either shred or pound it, in order to look well. You must put lobster, trout, char, pigeons and wild fowl whole into your pot, covered with clarified butter.

Of PICKLING.

RULES *to be observed in* PICKLING.

LET your brass pans, for green pickles, be exceeding bright and clean, otherwise your pickles will have no colour; use the very best and strongest white wine vinegar; likewise be very exact in watching when your pickles begin to boil, and change colour, so that you may take them off the fire immediately, otherwife they will lofe their colour, and grow foft in keeping. Cover your pickling jars with a wet bladder, and leather. All pickles fhould be kept in a cool dry place; if damp, it will quite fpoil them. When you ufe the pickles, take them out with a fpoon, and do not put in your fingers, for that will make them mothery.

To pickle Walnuts.

Make a pickle of falt and water, ftrong enough to bear an egg, boil and fcum it well, and pour it over your walnuts, let them ftand twelve days, changing the pickle at the end of fix days, then pour them into a cullender, and dry them with a coarfe cloth; then get the beft white wine vinegar, with cloves, mace, nutmeg, Jamaica corns, and fliced ginger, boil up thefe and pour it fcalding hot upon your walnuts; you may add fome fhallot, and a clove or two of garlick. To one hundred of walnuts, you muft put a pint of muftard feed; when they are cold put them into a jar, and cover them clofe.

To pickle Walnuts green.

Gather walnuts when they are fo tender that you can run a pin through them, pare and put them in water, let them lie four or five days, ftirring them twice a day to take out the bitter, then put them in ftrong falt and water, let them lie a week or ten days, ftirring them as before, then put them in frefh falt and water, and hang them over a fire; put to them a little allum, cover them up clofe with vine leaves, and let them hang over a flow fire till they are green, but be fure you don't let them boil: and when they are green put them into a fieve to drain; then take a little good alegar, put to it a little long pepper, a few bay leaves, a little horfe-radifh, a handful or two of muftard-feed, a little Jamaica pepper, a little falt, and fome rockambol if you have any, if not a few fhalots; boil all up together, put it to your walnuts, and let it ftand three or four days, giving them a fcald once a day, then tie them up for ufe. A fpoonful of this pickle is good for fifh fauce, or a calf's head hafh.

To

To make Mangoes.

Take your mangoes or cucumbers and cut a hole on the top, and put out the core and seeds; then fill it up with mustard-seed, garlick, and bits of horse-radish and ginger; fasten the tops with a small skewer, set them upright in a deep pot, and make your pickle thus: To a gallon of vinegar put in one handful of salt, some cloves, mace, and six races of ginger, and whole pepper; boil it up, put in a bit of dill, and then pour in your pickle boiling hot, and cover them down close; do this every other day three times.

To pickle large Cucumbers in slices.

Gather them before they are ripe, slice them into a pewter dish, to every dozen cucumbers slice two large onions thin, with a handful of salt between every row, then cover them with a pewter dish, and let them stand twenty-four hours, then put them into a cullendar, and let them drain very well; put them into a jar, cover them with white wine vinegar, and let them stand four hours; pour the vinegar from them into a copper sauce-pan, and boil it with a little salt; put to your cucumbers a little mace, whole pepper, a large race of ginger sliced, and then pour the boiling vinegar on; cover them close, and when they are cold tie them down. They will be fit to eat in two or three days.

To pickle Girkins.

Take girkins of the finest growth, pick them clean, put them in strong salt and water, let them lie a week or ten days whilst they be thoroughly yellow, then scald them in the same salt and water they lie in, scald them once a day, and let them lie till they are green, then set them at the corner end, and close covered.

To pickle Onions.

Peel some small white onions, and boil them among salt and water, and a little milk for a minute; strain them on a sieve, rub them in a cloth till they are quite dry, and when they are cold, put them into wide-mouthed bottles, fill them up with the best double-distilled

distilled vinegar, a sliced nutmeg, mace, white pepper, and a little salt, cork them down, and cover them over with a bladder.

To pickle Mushrooms.

The small button mushroom is preferable; lay them in milk and water, and rub them with a flannel; then put on a sauce-pan with water and salt, and when it boils put them in, and boil them two minutes; then take them out and lay them on a cloth to drain; when cold, put them in bottles with a little mace, white pepper, and nutmeg sliced; fill the bottles with the best double-distilled vinegar, cork them down tight, and tie a piece of bladder over them. You may put some sweet oil on the tops to preserve them.

To pickle Grapes or Barberries.

Put them into a pot, boil verjuice with a good quantity of salt, and let it stand till it is cold, and then put them in, and cover them.

To pickle Currants.

Take them before they are ripe; you must not take them from the stalk; make a pickle of salt and water, and a little vinegar, so keep them for use. They are proper for garnishing.

To pickle white Cabbage.

You may do it in quarters, or shave it in slices, and scald it about four minutes in water and salt, then take it out and cool it, boil up some vinegar and salt, whole pepper, mace, and ginger; when your pickle is boiled and skimmed put it to your cabbage, cover it directly, and it will keep white.

To pickle red Cabbage.

Cut off the stalks and outside leaves, and shred the remainder into a cullendar, throw salt upon it in shredding, and after it has drained two or three hours, put it into a jar, then make a pickle of vinegar, cloves, mace, ginger and sliced nutmeg, and boil it. When it is cold pour it over the cabbage, and it will be fit for use in twelve hours. If for keeping, pour it on hot, and stop it up close.

To

To pickle the fine purple Cabbage, so much admired at the great tables.

Take two cauliflowers, two red cabbages, have a peck of kidney beans, six sticks, with six cloves of garlick on each stick; wash all well, give them a boil up, then drain them, and lay them leaf by leaf upon a large table, and salt them with bay-salt, let them dry in the sun, or in a slow oven, until as dry as cork; then take a gallon of the best vinegar, one quart of water, a handful of salt, and an ounce of pepper; boil them, let it stand till it is cold; then take a quarter of a pound of ginger, cut it in pieces, salt it, let it stand a week; take half a pound of mustard-seed, wash it and lay it to dry, when very dry, bruise half of it; when all is ready for a jar, lay a row of cabbage, a row of cauliflowers and beans, and throw betwixt every row your mustard-seed, black pepper, ginger, and Jamaica pepper, mix an ounce of the root of turmerick powdered; put in the pickle, which must go over all. It is best when it hath been two years made, though it may be used the first year.

To pickle Rock Samphire.

Let the rock samphire be fresh picked, and not bruized; wash it clean, cut off the roots, tie it up in small bunches, put it into a brass-pan with a cabbage leaf under and over it, fill it up with one half alegar and the other half hard water, and set it on the fire till it is quite hot; hang it a little higher, and keep it hot till it is quite green; then take it out, drain it, and put it into a jar. Put some white wine vinegar into a sauce-pan with some black and clove pepper, and some rice ginger; set it on the fire, let it boil five minutes, pour it on the samphire, and cover it close down.

To make Catchup.

Take large mushrooms when they are fresh gathered, cut off the dirty ends, break them small in your hands, put them in a stone-bowl with a handful or two of salt, and let them stand all night; if you do not get mushrooms enough at once, with a little salt they

they will keep a day or two whilſt you get more, ſo put them into a ſtew-pot, and ſet them in a quick oven to bake for one hour; when they are enough ſtrain from them the liquor, and add black and clove pepper, mace, and cloves, in all half an ounce, and a little common ſalt; boil it for half an hour pretty quick, then put it into a mug; when it is cold, bottle it up, and keep it for uſe.

To pickle Pork.

Bone your pork, cut it into pieces, of a ſize fit to lie in the tub or pan you deſign it to lie in, rub your pieces well with ſalt-petre, then take two parts of common ſalt, and two of bay-ſalt, and rub every piece well; lay a layer of common ſalt in the bottom of your veſſel, cover every piece over with common ſalt, lay them one upon another as cloſe as you can, filling the hollow place on the ſides with ſalt; as your ſalt melts on the top, ſtrew on more, lay a coarſe cloth over the veſſel, a board over that, and a weight on the board to keep it down. Keep it cloſe covered; it will keep the whole year thus ordered. Put a pound of ſalt-petre and two pounds of bay-ſalt to a hog.

A pickle for Pork which is to be eat ſoon.

Take two gallons of pump-water, one pound of bay-ſalt, one pound of coarſe ſugar, ſix ounces of ſalt petre; boil all together, and ſkim it when cold; cut the pork in pieces, lay it down cloſe, and pour the liquor over it; cover it cloſe from the air, and it will be fit to uſe in a week. If you find the pickle begins to ſpoil, boil it again, and ſkim it; when cold your it on your pork.

To make Mutton Hams.

Take a hind-quarter of mutton, cut it like a ham, take one ounce of ſalt-petre, a pound of coarſe ſugar, and a pound of common ſalt; mix them and rub your ham, lay it in a hollow tray with the ſkin downwards, baſte it every day for a fortnight, then roll it in ſaw-duſt, and hang it in wood ſmoke a fortnight, then boil it, and hang it in a dry place, and cut it out in raſhers.   *To*

To make Bacon.

Take a side of pork, take off all the inside fat, lay it on a long board, that the blood may run away; rub it well with good salt on both sides, let it lie thus a week, then take a pint of bay-salt, a quarter of a pound of salt-petre, beat them fine, two pounds of coarse sugar, and a quarter of a peck of common salt; rub your pork well with the above ingredients, lay the skinny side downwards, and balle it every day with the pickle for a fortnight, then hang it in wood smoke for a month, and afterwards hang it in a dry place, but not too hot. All hams and bacon should hang clear from every thing, and not against a wall. Wipe off all the old salt before you put it into this pickle, and never keep them in a hot kitchen, or in a room where the sun comes, it makes them all rusty.

To salt Tongues.

Clean them, and cut off the root, then take two ounces of salt-petre, a quarter of a pound of bay-salt well beaten, salt them very well, and let them lie a a month or so, with the skinny side downwards. You may do a rump of beef the same way.

To pickle Mackrel, called Caveach.

Cut your mackrel into round pieces, and divide one into five or six pieces. To six large mackrel you may take one ounce of beaten pepper, three large nutmegs, a little mace, and a handful of salt, mix your salt and beaten spice together, then make two or three holes in each piece, and thrust the seasoning into the holes with your finger, rub the piece all over with the seasoning, fry them brown in oil, and let them stand till they are cold; then put them into vinegar, and cover them with oil. They will keep well covered a great while, and are very delicious.

To pickle Herrings.

Scald and clean them, take out the milts and roans, skewer them round, season them with salt and pepper, put them in a deep pot, cover them with alegar, put to them a little whole Jamaica pepper, and two or three bay-leaves; bake them, and keep them for ufe.

To pickle Oysters, Cockles, and Muffels.

Take two hundred oyfters, the frefheft you can get, fave the liquor as you open them, cut off the black verge, faving the reft, put them into their own liqour, then put the liquor and oyfters into a kettle, boil them gently half an hour, fkimming them as the fkum rifes, then take them of, take out the oyfters, ftrain the liquor through a cloth, then put in the oyfters again; then take out a pint of the liquor whilft it is hot, put to it three quarters of an ounce of mace, and half an ounce of cloves; juft give it a boil, then put it to the oyfters, and ftir up the fpices well among the oyfters, put in a fpoonful of falt, three quarters of a pint of the beft white wine vinegar, and a quarter of an ounce of whole pepper; let them ftand till they be cold, then put in the oyfters, as many as you well can, into the barrel, put in as much liquor as the barrel will hold, letting them fettle a while, and they will foon be fit to eat; or you may put them into ftone jars, cover them clofe with a bladder and leather, and be fure they are quite cold before you cover them up. Thus do cockles and muffels, only this, cockles are fmall, and to this fpice you muft have at leaft two quarts, nor is there any thing to pick off them. To muffels you muft have two quarts, take great care to pick the crab out under the tongue, and a little fus which grows at the root of the tongue. The two latter, cockles and muffels, muft be wafhed in feveral waters, to clean them from the grit; put them into a flew-pan, cover them clofe, and when they are open, pick them out of the fhells, and ftrain the liquor.

To pickle Shrimps.

Take the largeft you can get, pick them, boil them in a gill of water, or as much water as will cover them, according as you have a quantity of fhrimps, ftrain them through a hair fieve, then put to the liquor

quor a little spice, mace, whole pepper, white wine, white wine vinegar, and a little salt; boil these all together very well; when it is cold put in your shrimps, and they are fit for use.

To pickle Smelts.

Take a quarter of a peck of smelts, half an ounce of pepper, half an ounce of nutmeg, half an ounce of salt-petre, a quarter of an ounce of mace, and a quarter of a pound of common salt; beat all very fine, wash and clean the smelts, gut them, lay them in rows in a jar, and between each layer of smelts strew the seasoning, with or five bay-leaves, then boil red wine, and pour over as much as will cover them; then cover them with a plate, and when cold tie them down close. They exceed anchovies.

To pickle Salmon.

Take a salmon, and split it down the back, cut it across into four lengths, wash them clean, but do not take off the scales; have ready a kettle with boiling water, boil it three quarters of an hour, take it up, and set it to cool; add three quarts of vinegar to three quarts of the liquor it was boiled in, with a quarter of an ounce of cloves, a quarter of an ounce of mace, half an ounce of black pepper, two ounces of ginger cut in slices, a little bay salt, and two handfuls of common salt, boil them all well together one quarter of an hour, let it stand till it is cold, put your salmon into a kit, and pour your pickle over it.

Of PRESERVING.

To preserve Cherries with their leaves and stalks green.

FIRST dip the stalks and leaves in the best vinegar boiling hot, stick the sprig upright in a sieve till they are dry; in the mean time boil some double-refined sugar to syrup, and dip the cherries, stalks, and leaves in the syrup, and just let them scald; lay them on a sieve, and boil the sugar to a candy height,

height, then dip the cherries, ſtalks, leaves, and all, then ſtick the branches in ſieves, and dry them as you do other ſweetmeats. They look very pretty at candle-light in a deſert.

To make Marmalade of Apricots.

Stone your apricots, as many as you chuſe, put them immediately into a ſkellet of boiling water, keep them under till they are ſoft, then wipe them with a cloth, weigh your ſugar with your apricots, weight for weight, then diſſolve your ſugar in water, and boil it a candy height; then put in your apricots, being a little bruiſed; let them boil a quarter of an hour, then glaſs them up.

To preſerve Apricots.

Take your apricots, ſtone and pare them thin, and take their weight in double-refined ſugar beaten and ſifted, put your apricots in a ſilver cup or tankard, cover them over with ſugar, and let them ſtand ſo all night. The next day put them in a preſerving-pan, ſet them on a gentle fire, and let them ſimmer a little while, then let them boil till tender and clear, taking them off ſometimes to turn and ſkim. Keep them under the liquor as they are doing, and with a ſmall clean bodkin or great needle job them ſometimes, that the ſyrup may penetrate into them. When they are enough, take them up, and put them in glaſſes. Boil and ſkim your ſyrup; and when it is cold, put it on your apricots.

A nice way to preſerve Peaches.

Put your peaches in boiling hot water, juſt give them a ſcald, but do not let them boil, take them out and put them in cold water, then dry them in a ſieve, and put them in long wide mouthed bottles; to half a dozen peaches take a quarter of a pound of ſugar, clarify it, pour it over your peaches, and fill the bottles with brandy. Stop them cloſe, and keep them in a cloſe place.

To bottle Gooſeberries.

Gather your gooſeberries young, pick and bottle them,

them, put in the cork loofe, fet them in a pan of water, with a little hay in the bottom, put them into the pan when the water is cold, let it ftand on a flow fire, and mind when they are codled; do not let the pan boil, if you do it will break the bottles; when they are cold faften the cork, and put on a little rofin, fo keep them for ufe.

To bottle Damfins.

Take your damfins before they are full ripe, gather them when the dew is off, pick off the ftalks, and put them into dry bottles; do not fill your bottles over full, and cork them clofe, keep them in a cellar, and cover them over with fand.

To preferve Goofeberries whole without ftoning.

Take the largeft preferving goofeberries, and pick off the back eye, but not the ftalk, then fet them over the fire in a pot of water to fcald, cover them very clofe to fcald, but not boil or break, and when they are tender take them up into cold water; then take a pound and a half of double-refined fugar to a pound of goofeberries, and clarify the fugar with water, a pint to a pound of fugar, and when your fyrup is cold, put the goofeberries fingle in your preferving-pan, put the fyrup to them, and fet them on a gentle fire; let them boil, but not too faft, left they break; and when they have boiled, and you perceive that the fugar has entered them, take them off; cover them with white paper, and fet them by till the next day. Then take them out of the fyrup, and boil the fyrup till it begins to be ropy; fkim it, and put it to them again, then fet them on a gentle fire, and let them preferve gently, till you perceive the fyrup will rope; then take them off, fet them by till they are cold, cover them with paper, then boil fome goofeberries in fair water, and when the liquor is ftrong enough, ftrain it out. Let it ftand to fettle, and to every pint take a pound of double refined fugar, then make a jelly of it, put the goofeberries in glaffes when they are cold; cover them with the jelly the next day, paper them wet, and then half dry the paper that

goes

goes in the infide, it clofes down better, and then white paper over the glafs. Set it in your ftove, or a dry place.

To preferve the large green Plumbs.

Firft dip the ftalks and leaves in boiling vinegar, when they are dry have your fyrup ready, and firft give them a fcald, and very carefully with a pin take off the fkin; boil your fugar to a candy height, and dip in your plumbs, hang them by the ftalk to dry, and they will look finely tranfparent, and by hanging that way to dry, will have a clear drop at the top. You muft clear your fugar nicely.

To preferve Damfins.

You muft take fome damfins and cut them in pieces, put them in a fkillet over the fire, with as much water as will cover them. When they are boiled and the liquor pretty ftrong, ftrain it out; add for every pound of the whole damfins wiped clean, a pound of fingle-refined fugar, put the third part of your fugar into the liquor, fet it over the fire, and when it fimmers, put in the damfins. Let them have one good boil, and take them off for half an hour covered up clofe; then fet them on again, and let them fimmer over the fire after turning them, then take them out and put them in a bafon, ftrew all the fugar that was left on them, and pour the hot liquor over them. Cover them up, and let them ftand till next day, then boil them up again till they are enough. Take them up, and put them in pots; boil the liquor till it jellies, and pour it on them when it is almoft cold, fo paper them up.

To keep Barberries for Tarts all the year.

Take barberries when they are full ripe, and pick them from the ftalk, put them into dry bottles, cork them up very clofe, and keep them for ufe. You may do craneberries the fame way.

To preferve Barberries.

Take berries when full ripe and ftrip them, take their weight in fugar, and as much water as will wet your fugar, give it a boil and fkim it; then put in your

your berries, let them boil whilſt they look clear and your ſyrup thick, ſo put them into a pot; and when cold cover them up with a paper dipped in brandy.

To preſerve Fruit green all the year.

Gather your fruit when they are three parts ripe, on a very dry day, when the ſun ſhines on them, then take earthen pots with corks, or bung them that no air can get into them, dig a place in the earth a yard deep, ſet the pots therein, and cover them with the earth very cloſe, and keep them for uſe. When you take any out, cover them up again as at the firſt.

To preſerve Currants.

Take the weight of the currants in ſugar, pick out the ſeeds; take to a pound of ſugar, half a jack of water, let it melt, then put in your fruit, and let them do leiſurely, ſkim them, take them up, let the ſyrup boil, them put them on again; when they are clear, and the ſyrup thick enough, take them off, and when they are cold put them up in glaſſes.

To preſerve Raſpberries.

Gather them not too ripe, take their weight in ſugar, wet your ſugar with a little water, and put in your berries, let them boil ſoftly, and take care you do not break them; when they are clear take them up, boil the ſyrup till it be thick enough, then put them in again, and when cold put them up in glaſſes.

To keep Aſparagus or green Peas a year.

Green them as you do cucumbers, and ſcald them as you do other pickles made of ſalt and water; let it be always new pickle, and when you would uſe them, boil them in freſh water.

Artichokes preſerved the Spaniſh way.

Take the largeſt you can get, cut the tops of the leaves off, waſh them well and drain them, to each artichoke pour in a large ſpoonful of oil, ſeaſoned with pepper and ſalt; ſend them to the oven, and bake them, and they will keep a year.

Of CANDYING.

To boil Sugar to a candy height.

PUT a pound and a half of double refined sugar into a preserving pan, and put to it three quarters of a pint of water; set it over a clear fire, when it boils, skim it clean as it rises; when it begins to look clear and candies about the edges of the pan, it will then be high enough for any kind of fruit.

To candy Oranges, Lemons, and Citron.

Drain them clean from the syrup, wash them in luke-warm water, and lay them on a sieve to drain; then take as much clarified sugar as will cover what you will candy, and boil it till it blows very strong, then put in your rings, and boil them till it blows again; then take it from the fire, and let it cool a little; then with the back of a spoon rub the sugar against the inside of your pan, till you see the sugar becomes white; then with a fork take out the rings one by one, and lay them on a wire-grate to drain; then put in your faggots and boil them, rub the sugar, and take them up in bunches, cut them with a pair of scissars to what bigness you please, laying them on your wire to drain. Thus you candy all sorts of oranges and lemon peel, or chips.—Lemon rings and faggots are done the same way, with this distinction only, that the lemons ought to be pared twice over, that the ring may be the whiter; so you will have two sorts of faggots. But you must be sure to keep the outward from the other, else it will discolour them.

To candy Cherries.

Gather and stone them before they are full ripe, and having boiled your fine sugar to a height, pour it on them, gently moving them, and so let them stand till almost cold, take them out, and dry them by the fire.

To candy Barberries and Grapes.

Take preserved barberries, wash off the syrup in water, and sift fine sugar on them; then let them be dried in the stove, turning them from time to time, till they are thorough dry. Preserved grapes may also be candied after the same manner.

To candy Orange or Lemon-peels.

Having steeped your orange-peel, as often as you shall judge convenient in water, to take away the bitterness; let them be gently dried and candied with syrup made of sugar.

To candy Apricots.

You must slit them on one side of the stone, and put fine sugar on them; then lay them one by one on a dish, and bake them in a pretty hot oven; then take them out of the dish, and dry them on glass plates in an oven for three or four days.

To make Barley Sugar.

Boil barley water, strain it through a hair-sieve, then put the decoction into clarified sugar, brought to a candy height, or the last degree of boiling, then take it off the fire, and let the boiling settle, then pour it upon a marble stone rubbed with the oil of olives; when it cools, and begins to grow hard, cut it into pieces, and rub into lengths as you please.

To make Lemon Drops.

Take a pound of loaf sugar, beat and sift very fine, grate the rind of a lemon and put it to your sugar; take the whites of three eggs and whisk them to a froth, squeeze in some lemon to your taste, beat them for half an hour, and drop them on white paper; be sure you let the paper be very dry, and sift a little fine sugar on the paper before you drop them. If you would have them yellow, take a pennyworth of gambouge, steep it in some rose-water, mix to it some whites of eggs, and a small quantity of sugar, so drop them, and bake them in a slow oven.

To make Conserve of Red Roses, or any other Flowers.

Take rose-buds or any other flowers, and pick them, cut off the white part from the red, and put the red flowers and sift them through a sieve to take out the seeds; then weigh them, and to every pound of flowers take two pounds and a half of loaf sugar; beat the flowers in a pretty fine stone mortar, then by degrees put the sugar to them, and beat it very well till

till it is well incorporated together; then put it in your gallipots, tie it over with a paper, over that a leather, and it will keep seven years.

To make Syrup of Roses.

Infuse three pounds of damask rose-leaves in a gallon of warm water, in a well glazed earthen pot, with a narrow mouth, for eight hours, which stop close, that none of the virtue may exhale; when they have infused so long, heat the water again, squeeze them out, and put in three pounds more of rose-leaves, to infuse for eight hours more, then press them out very hard; then to every quart of this infusion add four pounds of fine sugar, and boil it to a syrup.

To make Conserve of Hips.

Gather hips before they grow soft, cut off the heads and stalks, slit them in halves, take out all the seeds and white that is in them very clean, then put them into an earthen pan, and stir them every day, or they will grow mouldy. Let them stand till they are soft enough to rub through a coarse hair sieve, as the pulp comes take it off the sieve; they are a dry berry, and will require pains to rub them through; then add its weight in sugar, mix them well together, without boiling, and keep it in deep gallipots for use.

CAKES, CHEESECAKES, CUSTARDS, &c.

To make a Pound Cake.

TAKE a pound of butter, beat it in an earthen pan with your hand one way, till it is like a thick cream, then have ready twelve eggs, only six whites, and beat them up with the butter, beat in a pound of sugar, a pound of flour, and a few carraway seeds; beat all well together for an hour, butter your tin, then put in the cake, and bake it an hour in a quick oven. Some like a pound of currants in it.

To make a Plumb Cake.

Take half a peck of flour, half a pint of rose water, a pint of cream, a pint of ale yeast, boil it, then add a pound and a half of butter, six eggs without the whites,

whites, four pounds of currants, half a pound of sugar, a nutmeg, and a little salt, work it very well, and let it stand an hour by the fire; then work it again, and bake it an hour and a half. Take care the oven be not too hot.

To make an exceeding fine Plumb Cake.

Take a quarter of a peck of the best flour, dry it, wash and pick clean three pounds of currants, set them before the fire to dry, half a pound of blanched almonds, beaten fine with rose-water, half a pound of raisins of the sun, washed, stoned and shred small, a pound of butter melted with a pint of cream, but it must not be put in hot, half a pint of ale-yeast, a pennyworth of saffron steeped in a pot of sack, ten or twelve eggs, half the whites, a quarter of an ounce of cloves and mace, one large nutmeg grated, a few carraway seeds, candied orange, citron, and lemon-peel sliced; you must make it thin, or there must be more butter and cream; perfume it with ambergrease, tied in a muslin bag, and steeped in the sack all night.

Iceing for a Plumb Cake.

Beat a pound and a half of treble-refined sugar, sift it through a fine sieve, and put it into a bowl, with the whites of five eggs well whisked, a bit of gum dragon (half the size of a nutmeg) dissolved in rose-water; whisk it an hour till it grows white and thick; if it is thin, it will run off the cake. When the cake is baked, take it out of the pan, and put it on a tin, then spread on half of the icing with a knife dry it in the oven, take it out, and spread on the other half, then dry it as before. This will make it look much whiter than laying it on at once.

To make a Butter Cake.

You must take a dish of butter, and beat it like cream with your hands, two pounds of fine sugar well beat, three pounds of flour well dried, and mix them in with the butter, 24 eggs, leave out half the whites, and then beat all together for an hour. Just as you put it into the oven, put in a quarter of ounce of mace, a nutmeg beat, a little sack or brandy, and seeds or currants, just as you please.

To make a good Seed Cake.

Take two pounds of butter beaten to a cream, a quarter of a peck of flour, a pound and three quarters of fine sugar, three ounces of candied orange-peel and citron, one ounce of carraway-seeds, ten eggs, and but five whites, a little rose-water, a few cloves, mace, and nutmeg, some new yeast, and half a pint of cream, then bake it in a hoop, and butter your paper; when it is baked, ice it over with the whites of eggs and sugar, and set it in the oven again to harden.

To make a light Seed Cake.

Take half a quarter of a peck of flour, some ginger, three eggs well beat, three spoonfuls of ale yeast, half a pound of butter, and six ounces of fine smooth carraway seeds, and work it warm together with your hand.

To make a cheap Seed Cake.

Put a pound and a half of butter in a sauce-pan, with a pint of new milk, set it on the fire, take a pound of sugar, half an ounce of all all-spice beat fine, and mix them with half a peck of flour. When the butter is melted, pour the butter and milk in the middle of the flour and work it up like paste. Pour in with the milk half a pint of good ale yeast, and set it before the fire to rise, just before it goes to the oven. You may either put in carraway seeds or currants, and bake it in a quick oven.

N. B. If you make two cakes they will take an hour and a half baking.

To make little fine Cakes.

One pound of flour, half a pound of sugar, beat half a pound of butter with your hand, mix all well together, and bake it in little cakes.

To make Shrewsberry Cakes.

Take two pounds of flour, a pound of sugar, finely searched, mix them together, (take out a quarter of a pound to roll them in) take four eggs beat, four spoonfuls of cream, and two spoonfuls of rose-water;

beat

beat them well together, and mix them with the flour into a paſte, roll them into thin cakes, and bake them in a quick oven.

To make Queen Cakes.

Take one pound of butter, three quarters of a pound of ſugar beaten and ſifted, put it down before the fire to warm, then beat it for half an hour; put in one pound of fine flour, eight eggs well whiſked, a nutmeg, and cinnamon beaten, a few almonds ſhred, and one pound of currants; mix it well together, butter ſome ſmall pans and put it in, with a bit of lemon and orange peel on the top, and a little ſugar duſted on them, then bake them fifteen minutes in a moderate oven. Make them without currants, if you chuſe.

To make Wigs.

Rub ten ounces of butter, and ten ounces of ſugar into three pounds and a half of flour, till it is like grated bread, adding to it a little nutmeg, and a few carraway ſeeds; make a hole in the middle, and put in half a pint of thick ale yeaſt, three eggs, and as much warm milk as will make it into a light paſte; roll it out, and make it into eighteen wigs; ſet them on tins, a little diſtance from the fire, (for one hour) to riſe, then bake them in a quick oven.

To make Bath Cakes.

Take two pounds and a half of flour, rub into it three quarters of a pound of freſh butter, and half a pound of ſugar; rub it till it is like grated bread; add three quarters of a pound of currants waſhed and dried, grate into it half a rice of ginger, half a nutmeg, three eggs beaten, half a pint of thick ale yeaſt, and four ſpoonfuls of ſack; then make a hole in the middle of the flour, put in the yeaſt and eggs, and as much warm milk as will make it into a light paſte; make it into eighteen little cakes, put them on tins, ſet them in a warm place to riſe, waſh them over with egg, ſtrew them over with carraway comfits, and bake them in a quick oven for half an hour.

To make Pepper Cakes.

Take half a gill of sack, half a quarter of an ounce of whole white pepper, put it in and boil it together a quarter of an hour, then take the pepper out, and put in as much double-refined sugar as will make it like a paste, then drop it in what shape you please on plates, and let it dry itself.

To make Ginger-bread Cakes or Nuts.

Take three pounds and a half of flour, three ounces of rice ginger beaten and sifted, three ounces of carraway seeds bruised, and three quarters of a pound of sugar; mix them well together, make a hole in the middle, melt three quarters of a pound of butter in a sauce-pan, put to it three pounds and a half of treacle; let it just warm, put it into your flour with four eggs, beat it well for half an hour with a wooden spoon, then put into it half a pound of lemon and orange peel; butter the cake-pan, put it in, and bake it in a soaking oven two hours and a half. You may let stand to cool, then make it into nuts, and bake them on tins.

To make Mackeroons.

Take a pound of almonds, let them be well scalded, blanched, and thrown into cold water, then dry them in a cloth, and pound them in a mortar, moisten them with orange-flower water, or the white of an egg, lest they turn to oil; afterwards take an equal quantity of fine powder sugar, with three or four whites of eggs and some milk, beat all well together, and shape them on wafer-paper, with a spoon round. Bake them on tin.

To make Biscuits.

Beat up six eggs with two spoonfuls of rose-water and sack, then add a pound of sugar powdered, and a pound of flour; mix them into the eggs by degrees, and an ounce of coriander seeds, mix all well together, shape them on white thin paper, or tin moulds, in any form you please; beat the white of an egg, rub them over with a feather, and dust fine sugar over them; set them in a slow oven till they rise and come
to

to a good colour, take them out, and when you have done with the oven, if you have no stove to dry them in, put them into the oven again, and let them stand all night.

To make Buns.

Take two pounds of flour, a pint of yeast, put a little sack in the yeast, and three eggs beaten, knead all together with a little warm milk, a little nutmeg, and a little salt; then lay it before the fire till it rises very light, then knead in a pound of fresh butter, a pound of rough carraway comfits, and bake them in a quick oven, in what shape you please, on floured paper.

To make Cheese-Cakes.

Take the curd of a gallon of milk, three quarters of a pound of butter, two grated biscuits, two ounces of blanched almonds pounded with some orange-flower water, half a pound of currants, seven eggs, sugar and spice; beat it up with a little cream till it is very light, then fill your cheese-cakes.

To make Rice Cheese-Cakes.

Boil two quarts of cream or milk a little while, with whole mace and cinnamon, then take it off the fire, take out the spice, and put in half a pound of rice-flour, make it boil, stirring it together, then take it off, and beat the yolks of twenty-four eggs, set it on the fire again, and keep it continually stirring till it is as thick as curds; add half a pound of blanched almonds pounded, and sweeten it to your palate; or, if you chuse, you may put in half a pound of currants, picked and rubbed in a clean cloth.

To make Lemon Cheese-Cakes.

Take two large lemon peels, boil and pound them well together in a mortar, with about six ounces of loaf sugar, the yolks of six eggs, and half a pound of fresh butter; pound and mix all well together, and fill the patty-pans about half full. Orange cheese-cakes are done the same way, only you boil the peel in two or three waters, to take out the bitterness.

To make Almond Cheese-Cakes.

Take half a pound of jordan almonds, and lay them in cold water all night, the next morning blanch them in cold water; then take them out, dry them in a clean cloth, and beat them very fine in a little orange-flour water; then take six eggs, leave out four whites, beat and strain them, then half a pound of white sugar, with a little beaten mace; beat all well together in a marble mortar, take ten ounces of fresh butter, melt it, a little grated lemon-peel, beat them with the other ingredients, mix all well together, and fill your pans.

An excellent Paste for Custards.

Take a pound of flour, twelve ounces of butter, the yolks of four eggs, six spoonfuls of cream, mix them together, let them stand near twenty minutes, then work it up and down, and roll it very thin.

To make a Custard.

Boil a quart of cream or milk, with a stick of cinnamon, large mace, and a quartered nutmeg; when half cold, mix it with eight yolks of eggs, and four whites well beat, some sack, sugar, and orange-flower water; set all on the fire, and stir it till the froth rises, which skim off; then strain it, and fill your crusts, which should be first dried in the oven, and which you should prick with a needle before you dry them, to prevent their rising in blisters; or you may put it in cups, without the paste.

To make an Almond Custard.

Take a quart of cream, put it in a stew-pan with a stick of cinnamon, two blades of mace, and three laurel leaves; boil it, and set it to cool; blanch two ounces of sweet almonds, beat them fine in a marble mortar with rose-water, mix it with cream, and sweeten it to your taste; set it on a slow fire, stirring it till it grows thick; do not let it boil, for it will curdle; stir it till it is almost cold, and put it in the cups.

To make plain Cuſtards.

Take a quart of new milk, ſweeten it to your taſte, grate in a little nutmeg, beat up eight eggs well, leave out half the whites, ſtir them into the milk, and bake it in china diſhes; or put them in a kettle of boiling water, taking care the water does not come above half way up the baſons, for fear of its getting into them; you may add a glaſs of brandy, or ſome roſe-water in the making.

To make a Cream Cuſtard.

Grate the crumb of a penny loaf very fine, and mix it with a good piece of butter, and a quart of cream, beat the yolks of twelve eggs with cream, ſweeten them with ſugar, let them thicken over the fire, make your cuſtard ſhallow, bake them in a gentle oven, and when they are baked, ſtrew fine ſugar over them.

To make a Rice Cuſtard.

Firſt boil a quart of cream with a blade or two of mace, then put to it boiled ground rice, well beaten with the cream, mix them together, and ſtir them well all the while it boils; and when it is enough, take it off, and ſweeten it as you like, and put in a little roſe-water, and ſerve it cold.

SYLLABUBS, CREAMS, and FLUMMERY.

To make a fine Syllabub from the Cow.

SWEETEN a quart of cyder with double refined ſugar, grate a nutmeg into it; then milk the cow into your liquor, when you have added what quantity of milk you think proper, pour half a pint or more (in proportion to the quantity of ſyllabub you make) of the ſweeteſt cream over it.

A whipped Syllabub.

Take two porringers of cream and one of white wine, grate the ſkin of a lemon, take the whites of three eggs,

eggs, sweeten it to your taste, then whip it with a whisk, take off the froth as it rises, and put it in your syllabub glasses, and they are fit for use immediately.

To make a fine Cream.

Take a pint of cream, sweeten it to your palate, grate some nutmeg, put in a spoonful of orange-flower water, rose-water, and two spoonfuls of sack, beat up four eggs and two whites, stir it all together one way over the fire till it is thick, then pour it in cups.

Lemon Cream.

Take the juice of four large lemons, half a pint of water, a pound of double-refined sugar beaten very fine; mix all together and strain it, set it on a gentle fire, stirring it all the while, and skim it clean; put it into the peel of one lemon when it is very hot, but not to boil; take out the lemon-peel, and pour it into china dishes, and serve it up.

Orange Cream.

Take four large Seville oranges, grate off the rind, and put it in a bason with a pint of water, and the juice of the oranges; let it stand one hour, add six eggs, leaving out three yolks; whisk it all well together, strain it into a stew-pan, with as much sugar as will sweeten it; set it on the fire, stir it all the time, and when it grows thick, take it off, and serve it up in jelly glasses on a salver or desert frame, or in a glass bowl.

Raspberry Cream.

Put one pint and a half of cream into a china bowl, add to it half a tea spoonful of cochineal, to give it a colour, whisk it to raise a froth, and as it rises, take it off, and lay it on a sieve; when you have got as much froth as will serve to cover the cream, put into your bowl half a pound of rasp jam, mix it well together, strain it through a sieve to take the seeds quite out of it; put it into a glass bowl or deep china dish, and the froth over it. It is proper for a corner dish for a second course, or a middle dish for supper.

Whipped

Whipped Cream.

Take a quart of thick cream, the whites of eight eggs beaten with half a pint of fack; mix it together, fweeten it to your tafte with double-refined fugar; you may perfume it (if you pleafe) with mufk or ambergreafe tied in a rag, fleeped in the cream. Whip it up with a whifk, and a piece of lemon-peel tied in the middle of the whifk. Take off the froth with a fpoon, and lay it in your glaffes or bafons.

To make a Trifle.

Cover the bottom of a difh or bowl with Naples bifcuits broken in pieces, mackeroons broke in halves, and ratifia cakes. Juft wet them through with fack, then make a good boiled cuftard not too thick, and when cold pour it over them, then put a fyllabub over that. Garnifh with ratifia cakes, currant jelly, and flowers.

Flummery.

Take a large calf's foot, cut out the great bones and boil them in two quarts of water, then ftrain it off, and put to the clear jelly half a pint of thick cream, two ounces of fweet almonds, and an ounce of bitter almonds beaten together. Let it juft boil, and then ftrain it off; when it is as cold as milk from the cow, put it in cups or glaffes.

JELLIES and JAMS.

Calf's Feet Jelly.

BOIL two calves feet in a gallon of water, till it comes to a quart, then ftrain it, let it ftand till cold, skim off all the fat clean, and take the jelly up clean. If there is any fettling in the bottom, leave it; put the jelly into a fauce-pan, with a pint of mountain wine, half a pound of loaf fugar, the juice of four large lemons, beat up fix or eight whites of eggs with a whisk, then put them into a fauce-pan, and ftir all toge-

together well till it boils. Let it boil a few minutes. Have ready a large flannel bag, pour it in, it will run quick through, pour it in again till it runs clear, then have ready a large china bason, with the lemon-peels cut as thin as poſſible, let the jelly run into that bason; and the peels both give it a fine amber colour, and alſo a flavour; with a clean ſilver ſpoon fill your glaſſes.

Hartſhorn Jelly.

Take half a pound of hartſhorn, and put it into an earthen pan, with two quarts of ſpring water, cover it cloſe and ſet it in the oven all night, then ſtrain it into a pipkin with half a pound of double refined ſugar, half a pint of Rheniſh wine, the juice of three or four lemons, three or four blades of mace, and the whites of four or five eggs well beaten, and mix it ſo that it may not curdle. Set it on the fire till there ariſeth a thick ſcum, run it through a napkin or jelly bag, and turn it up again till it is all quite clear.

Raſpberry Jam.

Take a pint of currant jelly and a quart of raſpberries, bruiſe them well together, ſet them over a ſlow fire, ſtir it till it boils, let it boil five or ſix minutes, put it in your pots, and keep it for uſe.

Of MADE WINES, &c.

Obſervations on Made Wines.

BEFORE you begin to make wines, have all your utenſils abſolutely clean and ſweet, and make more than will fill your caſk, for it waſtes in working; and will require filling up. Let them be kept twelve months in the caſk. If at that time it is not fine, draw a pint, and put half an ounce of iſinglaſs into it, and let it ſtand four days to diſſolve, ſtirring it twice a-day; return it into the caſk, ſtirring it well about, and bung it very cloſe, though raiſe the ſpile to give it vent; the ſame do to every wine when bunged down, or the cask is in danger. When quite fine, bottle it, and put a piece of ſugar into each bottle; and follow your receipts in every other particular.

Gooſe-

Gooseberry Wine.

To eight gallons of water add thirty pounds of sugar, boil it for ten minutes; when it is near cold, add to it sixty pounds of ripe gooseberries bruized, with three spoonfuls of yeast; let it ferment for three days, strain it through a sieve, press the gooseberries dry, tun it into a cask, and add to it two quarts of brandy. When it has done fermenting, stop it close down for twelve months, then bottle it.

To make Orange Wine.

To five gallons of water put eighteen pounds of lump sugar, boil it for fifteen minutes, and put it into a clean tub; when it is near cold, add to it the juice of fifty oranges, the rinds of ten pared very thin, and a little yeast; let it ferment for two days, stirring it three times a day; then strain out the rind, and tun it with the juice of six lemons made into a syrup, with one pound of sugar; add two quarts of brandy; when it has done working, stop it close down, keep it twelve months, and bottle it.

To make Raspberry Wine.

Take some fine raspberries, bruise them with the back of a spoon, then strain them through a flannel bag into a stone jar. To each quart of juice put a pound of double-refined sugar, stir it well together, and cover it close; let it stand three days, then pour it off clear. To a quart of juice put two quarts of white wine, bottle it off; it will be fit to drink in a week. Brandy made thus is a very fine dram, and a much better way than steeping the raspberries.

To make Elder-flower Wine, very like Frontiniac.

Take six gallons of spring water, twelve pounds of white sugar, six pounds of raisins of the sun chopped. Boil these together one hour, then take the flowers of elder, when they are falling, and rub them off to the quantity of half a peck. When the liquor is cold, put them in, the next day put in the juice of three lemons, and four spoonfuls of good ale yeast. Let it stand covered up two days, then strain it off, and put it in a vessel fit for it. To every gallon of wine put a quart of Rhenish, and put your bung lightly on a fortnight, then stop it down close. Let it stand six months; and if you find it is fine, bottle it off.

To make Elder Wine to imitate Port.

Bake the elder berries, strain the juice through a sieve, and to a gallon of juice put four gallons of cyder and ten pounds of lump sugar, with a little yeast; let it ferment together three days, stirring it twice a day, and tun it into a cask that will just hold it; add to it one quart of brandy. When it has done fermenting, stop it close down for twelve months, and bottle it.—If the cyder be right good, it will drink very little inferior to Port wine.

To make Raisin Wine.

Pick thirty pounds of Malaga raisins clean from the stalks, chop them a little, put them in a tub, and pour on them five gallons of water; let them stand to ferment for ten days, strain them through a sieve, and press the raisins dry. Put it into a cask with a quart of brandy; when it is done fermenting, stop it close down, but do not put the peg too tight in.

To make Black Currant Wine.

Boil six gallons of water, put it into a tub, and when it is near cold, add to it thirty six pounds of black currants bruized; let them stand for two days, and strain the juice through a sieve; add to it twenty pounds of loaf sugar, and a little yeast; let it stand for three days, stirring it three times each day; tun it into a barrel, with two quarts of brandy; when it has done fermenting, stop it close down, keep it for twelve months, and then bottle it.

To make Balm Wine.

Boil four gallons of water with fourteen pounds of sugar for three quarters of an hour, and put it into a tub; add to it four pounds of the tops of balm when they are in flower; bruise them a little, put to it a little yeast, let it stand two days, then strain and tun it. When it has done working, put to it a pint and a half of brandy, stop it close down, keep it six months, then bottle it.

RULES for BREWING.

CARE must be taken in the first place to have the malt clean; and after it is ground, it ought to stand four or five days.

For strong October, five quarters of malt to three hogsheads, and twenty-four pounds of hops. This will afterwards make two hogsheads of good keeping small beer, allowing five pounds of hops to it.

For good middling beer, a quarter of malt makes a hogshead of ale, and one of small beer; or it will make three hogsheads of good small beer, allowing eight pounds of hops. This will keep all the year. Or it will make twenty gallons of strong ale, and two hogsheads of small beer that will keep all the year.

If you intend your ale to keep a great while, allow a pound of hops to every bushel; if to keep six months, five pounds to a hogshead; if for present drinking, three pounds to a hogshead, and the softest and clearest water you can get.

Observe the day before to have all your vessels very clean, and never use your tubs for any other use except to make wines.

Let your casks be very clean the day before with boiling water; and if your bung is big enough, scrub them well with a little birch broom or brush; but if they be very bad, take out the heads, and let them be scrubbed clean with a hand-brush and sand and fullers-earth. Put on the head again and scald them well, throw into the barrel a piece of unslacked lime, and stop the bung close.

The first copper of water, when it boils, pour into your mash-tub, let it be cool enough to see your face in; then put in your malt, and let it be well mashed, have a copper of water boiling in the mean time, and when your malt is well washed, fill your mashing-tub, stir it well again, and cover it over with the sacks. Let it stand three hours, then set a broad shallow tub under the cock, let it run very softly, and if it is thick throw it up again till it runs fine, then throw a handful of hops in the under tub, and let the mash run into it, and fill your tubs till all is run off. Have water boiling in the copper, and lay as much more on as you have occasion for, allowing one third for boiling and waste. Let that stand an hour, boiling more water to fill the mash-tub for small beer; let the fire down a little, and put it into tubs enough to fill your mash. Let the second mash be run off, and fill your copper with the first wort; put in part of your hops, and make it boil quick. About an hour is long enough; when it is half boiled, throw in a handful of salt. Have a clean white wand and dip it into the copper, and if the wort feels clammy, it is boiled enough; then slacken your fire, and take off your wort. Have ready a large tub, put two sticks acrofs, and set your straining basket over the tub on the sticks, and strain your wort through it. Put your other wort on to boil with the rest of the hops; let your mash be still covered again with water, and thin your wort that is cooled in as many things as you can; for the thinner it lies, and the quicker it cools, the better. When quite cool, put it into the tunning tub. Mind to throw a handful of salt into every boil. When the mash has stood an hour draw it off, then fill your mash with cold water, take off the wort in the copper, and order it as before. When cool, add to it the first in the tub; so soon as you empty one copper, fill the other, so boil your small beer well. Let the last mash run off, and when both are boiled with fresh hops, order them as the two first boilings; when cool, empty the mash-tub, and put the small beer to work there. When cool enough, work it, set a wooden bowl full of yeast in the beer, and it will work over with a little of the beer in the boil. Stir your tun up every twelve hours, let it stand two days, then tun it, taking off the yeast. Fill your vessels full, and save some to fill your barrels; let it stand till it has done working, then lay on your bung lightly for a fortnight, after that stop it as close as you can. Mind you have a vent-peg at the top of the vessel; in warm weather, open it, and if your drink hisses, as it often will, loosen it till it has done, then stop it close again. If you can boil your ale in one boiling it is best, if your copper will allow of it; if not, boil it as conveniency

niency ferves. The strength of your beer must be according to the malt you allow, more or less; there is no certain rule.

When you come to draw your beer, and find it is not fine, draw off a gallon, and set it on the fire, with two ounces of isinglass cut small and beat. Dissolve it in the beer over the fire; when it is all melted, let it stand till it is cold, and pour it in at the bung, which must lay loose on till it has done fermenting, then stop it close for a month.

Take great care your casks are not musty, or have any ill taste; if they have, it is the hardest thing in the world to sweeten them.

You are to wash your cask with cold water before you scald them, and they should lie a day or two soaking, and clean them well, then scald them.

⋙⋘⋙⋘⋙⋘⋙⋘⋙⋘⋙⋘

The Order of a Modern BILL of FARE for each Month, in the Manner the Dishes are to be placed upon the Table.

JANUARY.

First Course.

Cod's Head.

Scotch Collops.　　　　　　　　　　　Petit Patties.
Leg of Lamb.　Chesnut Soup.　Boiled Chickens.
Raisolds.　　　　　　　　　　　　　　Tongue.

Roast Beef.

Second Course.

Roasted Turkey.

Marinated Smelts.　　　　　　　　　Mince Pies.
Sweetbreads.　　Jellies.　　　　　　Larks.
Almond Cheesecakes.　　　　　　　　Lobsters.

Woodcocks.

FE-

FEBRUARY.

First Course.
Dish of Fish.

Chickens.
Ham.

Pea Soup.

Mutton Collops.
Rump of Beef
a la Daube.

Port Cutlets.
Sauce Robart.

French Pye.

Fillet of Veal.

Second Course.
Wild Fowls.

Cardoons.
Scollopt Oysters.
Tartlets.

Epergne.

Stewed Pippins.
Ragout Mellé.
Artichoke Bottoms.

Hare.

MARCH.

First Course.
Stewed Carp or Tench.

Sheeps Rumps.
Beef Steak Pye.
Veal Collops.

Soup Lorrain.

Fillet of Pork.
Almond Pudding.
Calves Ears.

Chine of Mutton and
Stewed Cellery.

Second Course.
A Poulard Larded.

Blancmange.
Ragou'd Sweet-
breads.
Crawfish.

A Trifle.

Prawns.
Fricasee of
Rabbits.
Stewed Pears.

Tame Pigeons.

APRIL.

APRIL.
First Course.

Crimp Cod and Smelts.

Boiled Chickens.		Cutlets a la Maintenon.
Pigeon Pye.	Spring Soup.	Beef Tremblong.
Lambs Tails a la Bashemel		Tongue.
	Loin of Veal.	

Second Course.
Ducklings.

Asparagus.		Black Caps.
Roast Sweetbreads.	Jellies and Syllabubs.	Oyster Loaves.
Tansey.		Mushrooms.
	Ribs of Lamb.	

MAY.
First Course.

Calvert's Salmon broiled.

Rabbits with Onions.		Collared Mutton.
Pigeon Pye raised.	Vermicelli Soup.	Maccaroni Trout.
Ox Palates.		Martelot of Tame Duck.
	Chine of Lamb.	

Second Course.
Green Goose.

Asparagus.		Cocks Combs.
Gooseberry Tarts.	Epergne.	Custards.
Lamb Cutlets.		Stewed Celery.
	Roast Chickens.	

JUNE.

(144)

JUNE.

First Course.

Turbot.

Chickens.		Harrico.
Lamb Pye.	Green Pea Soup.	Ham.
Veal Cutlets.		Orange Pudding.

Haunch of Venison.

Second Course.

Turkey Poults.

Pears.	Apricot Puffs.	Lobsters.
Fricasee of Lamb.	Fruit.	Roasted Sweetbreads.
Smelts.	Cherry Tart.	Artichokes.

Roasted Rabbits.

JULY.

First Course.

Mackarel, &c.

Breast of Veal a la Braise.		Pulpeton.
Venison Pasty.	Herb Soup.	Neck of Venison.
Chickens.		Mutton Cutlets.

Boiled Goose and
Stewed Red Cabbage.

Second Course.

Roast Turkey.

Stewed Peas.		Apricot Tart.
Sweetbreads.	Fruit.	Fricasee of Rabbits.
Custards.		Blaiz'd Pippins.

Roast Pigeons.

AUGUST.

AUGUST.

First Course.

Stewed Soals.

Fillets of Pigeons.   Turkey a la Daube.
French Patty.   Crawfish Soup.   Tongue.
Chickens.   Rolard of Beef
            Palates.

Fillet of Veal.

Second Course.

Roast Ducks.

Maccaroni.   Fillets of Soals.
Cheese Cakes.   Jellies.   Apple Pye.
Matelot of Eels.   Fricasee of
            Sweetbreads.

Leveret.

SEPTEMBER.

First Course.

Dish of Fish.

Chickens.   Veal Collops.
Pigeon Pye.   Gravy Soup.   Almond Tourt.
Harrico of Mutton.   Ham.

Roast Beef.

Second Course.

Wild Fowls.

Peas.   Ragou'd Lobsters.
Sweetbreads.   Fruit.   Fry'd Piths.
Crawfish.   Fry'd Artichokes.

Partridges.

OCTOBER.

First Course.

Cod and Oyster Sauce.

Jugged Hare.   Small Puddings.
French Patty.   Almond Soup.   Fillet of Beef
                                               larded and roasted.
Chickens.   Torrent de Veau.
              Tongue and Udder.

Second Course.

Pheasant.

Stewed Pears.   Mushrooms.
Roast Lobsters.   Jellies.   Oyster Loaves.
White Fricasee.   Pippins.

Turkey.

NOVEMBER.

First Course.

Dish of Fish.

Veal Cutlets.   Ox Palates.
Boiled Turkey   Vermicelli   Leg of Lamb
and Oyster Sauce.   Soup.   and Spinage.
Beef Collops.   Harrico.

Chine of Pork.

Second Course.

Woodcocks.

Sheeps Rumps.   Crocan.
Oyster Patty.   Fruit.   Ragou'd Lobsters
Blancmange.   Lambs Ears.

Hare.

DECEMBER.

DECEMBER.

First Course.
Cod's Head.

Chickens. Fricandau of Veal.
Pudding. Stewed Beef. Calves Feet Pye.
Fillet of Pork Tongue.
with sharp Sauce.

Chine of Lamb.

Second Course.
Wild Fowls.

Lambs Fry. Sturgeon.
Gallantine. Jellies. Savory Cake.
Prawns. Mushrooms.

Partridges.

⋙⋘⋙⋘⋙⋘⋙⋘⋙⋘⋙⋘⋙⋘

GRAVIES and SAUCES.

CUT some carrots, turnips, onions, sweet herbs, chabbots, some cloves, black and clove pepper, let your roots be cut in slices, put them in a stew-pan with a piece of butter, stir them over the fire with a wooden spoon for half an hour, let them be brown, put to it two quarts of boiling water, a handful of pease, and a few mushrooms; let it stew for one hour, strain it off, and use it under roasts, or in ragoos, and made dishes.

To make brown Gravy.

Cut three pounds of a leg of veal, and two pounds of lean beef, in thin slices, lay it in a stew-pan with one carrot, one turnip, one onion, and a bunch of sweet herbs, some whole black and clove pepper, set it on the fire to brown, have ready three quarts of boiling water, and when the bottom of the stew-pan is quite brown, (but not burnt) put in your water, and let it fimmer flowly for one hour and a half, then ftrain it, and keep it for ufe in a cool place.

To make white Gravy.

Put two pounds of a leg of veal into a ftew-pan, fet it on the fire to draw for ten minutes, but do not let it brown; add to it two quarts of water or broth, fome carrots, turnips, one onion, and a bunch of fweet herbs, fome whole pepper, mace, and cloves, fet it on the fire, and let it ftew for two hours, then ftrain it, and keep it for ufe in a cool place.

To make Cullis.

Take two pounds of a leg of veal, one pound of ham cut in flices, and an old hen, four large onions, two turnips, two carrots, a bunch of fweet herbs, and a little cellery, fome black and clove pepper, and mace, and fet them on the fire to draw; let your ftew-pan be quite brown, but not burnt, add to it three quarts of boiling water, let it ftew flowly for two hours, thicken it up with two fpoonfuls of flour, mixed with water, let it fimmer for five minutes, pafs it through a ftrainer with a wooden fpoon, fet it by in a mug, and keep it for ufe in a cool place.

Sauce for a Green Goofe.

Pound a handful of green wheat in a mortar, fqueeze the juice through a fieve into a ftew-pan, add a piece of fugar, and pour to it a quarter of a pint of thick melted butter, make it quite hot, add to it a quarter of a pint of green goofe berries fcalded, and ferve it up in a boat. If you have no wheat, green it with fpinage juice.

Sauce for roafted Venifon or Hare.

Take a little red wine and water, a ftick of cinnamon, a blade of mace, and a little grated white bread, let it ftew a little, add a bit of fugar, and ferve it up in a boat.

Currant

Currant Jelly Sauce for Venison.

Put half a pound of currant jelly in a stew-pan, with two tea cups full of red wine, let it boil for five minutes, stirring it all the time, pour it into a sauce-boat, and serve it up hot.

Gravy Sauce for Venison and Wild Fowl.

Put half a pint of brown gravy into a stew-pan, peal five shalots, cut them very fine, and put them into the gravy with two spoonfuls of vinegar, to give it a sharp taste, a little pepper and salt, put it into a boat, and serve it up hot.

Apple Sauce for a Stubble Goose or roast Pork.

Pare six apples, cut them into slices, and put them into a sauce-pan with some water, set them on the stove to stew gently; when they are tender, bruise them, add a little butter and sugar, stir them, put them into a sauce-boat, and serve it up hot.

Sauce for a Hare.

Chop two spoonfuls of capers very fine, put them into a stew pan with half a pint of brown gravy, a spoonful of soy or catchup, and a small piece of anchovy, let it simmer, add a little Cayen, and thicken it up with butter and flour; when your hare is roasted, dish it up with the sauce under it.

Sauce for roasted Rabbits.

Take their livers, cut off the gall, and boil them with a little parsley for one quarter of an hour, cut the parsley by itself, and the liver by itself, mix them together with some good melted butter; when your rabbits are roasted, dish them up with your sauce under them.

Sauce for boiled Carp or Tench.

Take half a pint of gravy, and two tea-cups full of red wine, two anchovies washed and chopped, two onions stuck with cloves, and a bit of horse-radish, let it simmer for a quarter of an hour, thicken it up with six ounces of butter, and a little flour, put it into a boat, and serve it up.

To make Anchovy Sauce.

Wash two anchovies clean, strip them from the bone, chop them very fine, put them into a stew-pan, with a tea-cup full of brown gravy, a quarter of a pound of fresh butter, some flour, a little lemon juice, a spoonful of soy, a bit of horse-radish, set it on the fire, and stir it all the time till it boils, take out the horse-radish, pour it into a boat, and serve it up.

Lobster Sauce.

Crack the shells of a boiled lobster, take out the meat, and cut it into dice half an inch square, put it into a stew-pan; if there is any spawn, pound it in a mortar, and put it to it, add six ounces of sweet butter, with a little flour, some gravy, a little juice of lemon, one anchovy, and a tea cup full of the liquor in which the fish was boiled, a blade of mace, and a little Cayen, boil them one minute, and serve them up in a sauce-boat.

Oyster Sauce.

Open sixty oysters, put them into a stew-pan, set them on the fire, and boil them for ten minutes, pour the liquor clear from the sediment into a stew-pan, beard and wash your oysters clean, and put them to it; add six ounces of butter, a little flour, and a little lemon juice, set it on the fire, and stir it till it boils, pour it into a sauce-boat, and serve it up, or pour it over boiled turkeys or fowls.

Shrimp Sauce.

Pick one gill of shrimps, wash them clean, put them into a stew-pan, with one anchovy cut very fine a tea-cup full of gravy, a quarter of a pound of butter, with a little flour, and some lemon juice, set it on the fire, stir it till it boils, put it in a sauce-boat, and serve it up.—Mussel and cockle sauce are made the same way.

An excellent Fish Sauce.

Take two tea-cups full of white veal gravy, add one spoonful of capers chopt fine, two slices of horse-radish, one onion, two cloves, and a quarter of an anchovy,

anchovy, set them on the fire, add a quarter of a pound of butter, and a little flour, let it just boil, put it into a sauce-boat, and serve it up.

White Sauce for Salt Fish.

Put half a pint of cream into a stew-pan, let it boil for ten minutes, throw in a little parsley shred fine, and a piece of butter and flour to thicken it, boil it five minutes, stirring it all the time; when your salt fish is boiled, lay it in your dish, with this sauce over it, and serve it up hot for a first course.

Egg Sauce for Salt Fish.

Boil six eggs hard, chop them, put them into half a pound of melted butter, let it just boil, put it into a boat, and serve it up.

Bread Sauce.

Put the crumbs of a halfpenny roll into a sauce-pan with some water and some pepper-corns, one onion cut in slices, two ounces of butter, let it boil till the bread is soft, beat it up, and add three spoonfuls of thick cream to make it white, let it just simmer, pour it in a boat, and serve it up. This is a proper sauce for roast turkey, pheasant, or partridge.

Cellery Sauce for roast Mutton.

Take the white ends of cellery, cut in lengths one inch and a half, let it simmer in boiling water for ten minutes, take it out, and put it into a stew pan, with half a pint of brown gravy, let it stew till tender, add a little pepper and salt, put it into your dish under roast mutton or veal.

Cucumber Sauce.

Take six large cucumbers, split them down the middle, and take out the seeds, cut them in lengths of one inch, and half an inch broad, add two onions cut small, then put a piece of butter into a stew-pan; when it is hot, put in your cucumber and onions, fry them for ten minutes, dust in a little flour, pepper and salt to your taste, add half a pint of brown gravy, let them stew till tender, skim off the fat, and serve them

them up hot in a sauce boat, or in a dish under roast mutton or veal.

Roe Boat Sauce.

Cut six large onions in small dice, then put three ounces of butter in a large stew-pan, when it is hot put in your onions, let them fry till they begin to grow brown, then dust in a little flour, and add half a pint of brown gravy, let them stew till tender, and skim off the fat; add a tea spoonful of made mustard, and a little pepper and salt to your taste.—This is an excellent sauce to turkey legs, broiled pigs ears, and neats feet.

To make Egg Sauce proper for roasted Chickens.

Melt your butter thick and fine, chop two or three hard-boiled eggs fine, put them into a bason, pour the butter over them, and have good gravy in the dish.

Chesnut Sauce.

Roast two dozen chesnuts, peal off the skin, put them into a little white gravy, let them stew slowly on a stove for half an hour, then pour in a quarter of a pint of melted butter, add a little sugar, and serve it up hot.

Sorrel Sauce for Turbit or Fricandoe.

Pick two handfuls of garden sorrel, wash it clean, boil it for four minutes in water, strain it off, and press the water from it, chop it fine, and put it in a stew-pan, with a piece of butter, a little flour, two tea-cups full of gravy, and a little pepper and salt, set it on the fire, and let it stew for ten minutes, stirring it all the time, pour it into a boat, and serve it up with boiled turbit.—This sauce is proper to put into a dish under fricandoes.

F I N I S.

www.ingramcontent.com/pod-product-compliance
Lightning Source LLC
Chambersburg PA
CBHW030318170426
43202CB00009B/1051